THE
BRIGHT
SIDE

(Even If You Have To Make It Up!)

Joe Bushue

INTRODUCTION

About 11 years ago as I was almost done writing my first book, A Cow on a Walker (available on Amazon), I sent two chapters to the column writer of our local newspaper. I asked her if she thought any of it would be "column worthy". She wrote back and told me that she thought I should get in contact with the editor of a monthly insert that went into all the Pamplin News Syndicate's 30+ local newspapers. She told me, based on what she saw, I could write a monthly column about how I was tolerating multiple sclerosis.

After we agreed the column could be about other things also, I started submitting monthly columns for her approval, which she quickly gave. I found that I could write more columns about other things that happened or that I "saw" and found in my mind somewhat humorous. As I got to writing all these, and also a few about MS, I realized that they all had one thing in common- if you look hard enough, or even sometimes invent it, in every situation you'll always find the bright side. That's what I named my column that ran monthly for over 10 years. This book is just a copy of the columns I've written over the years. Remember while reading this book, if you look hard enough, you'll always find the bright side.

The book is divided into different segments, in no particular order for no particular reason. These include the holidays, which I've always found a lot of humorous things about, living with some sort of personal handicap (such as MS), lawyers, doctors, computer illiteracy, and just some other things in general thrown in. Again, always look for the bright side. It's usually there, if not, pretend it is!

CHAPTER 1
GROWING UP (AND UP...)

Graduating from the kids' table to the 'Big Table'

Some milestones of life are known. You know exactly when your age becomes double digits, when you become a teenager at 13, and at 16 you can get a driver's license.

But one milestone of importance doesn't come at a set age. I finally was told that I could sit at the "Big Table" for Thanksgiving! I'd apparently done my time at that rickety old card table kind of stuck in the corner. I felt like I had arrived and had earned my seat with the adults. I could finally take part in some real conversation, enjoy the jokes and be a true participant in this family tradition. To tell the truth, I was pretty excited. I got to sit on the corner at the end of a long oak table set for 10!

I was between my great-aunt Martha and my dad's second cousin (I think) Henry. We all took our seats. Out came the turkey, and the meal started. I had to remind Aunt Martha several times just exactly who I was. Cousin Henry liked to tell anybody who would listen "Why the chicken crossed the road" jokes. He made sure you got them with a quick jab to your side. (I had no idea there were so many reasons.)

As the food started to get passed around the table, I learned that particular corner of the table was like the busiest intersection in New York's Times Square. I barely got my plate loaded before all the passing and polite requests started over. So much for the relaxed and pleasant adult conversation. The only jokes (for lack of a better term) were the chicken ones that Cousin Henry seemed to have an endless supply of.

I glanced over at my old kids' table and noticed that were all eating and laughing between bites, visiting and sharing info about what was happening with everyone else. So far all I had learned between passing the rolls and gravy was that Aunt Martha was lactose intolerant and that candied yams gave Cousin Henry gas.

I started to wonder what I had to do to earn my way back to the kids' table. So far, the "Big Table" wasn't at all like I thought it would be. It was kind of like when you were a kid and you wanted to watch your favorite cartoon show on TV but had to watch the news instead. You wondered what the big deal with the news was.

But as I got older, I realized that the news had more importance. I then decided I had graduated from the kids' table to the "big one" to become an official Family Thanksgiving Dinner apprentice. After a few years of learning the ropes, I too could someday become a journeyman. Just think: In a shorter amount of time than I had spent with the card table crowd, I would be a learned holiday dinner pro!

As I looked back at all the Thanksgiving feasts I was lucky enough to have enjoyed, and the anticipation in looking forward to it every year, I realized it was worth the wait. The kids' table was just the gateway to the apprentice training I would get at the "big one."

But I have to admit, sometimes that card table looked pretty good.

Regardless of where you sit this and every year, take time to realize all that we have to be thankful for and enjoy it. For everyone still at that rickety old table wondering when it'll be your turn to move on up, remember, your turn will come.

Wait, that's not real – that's TV

Does Mom wear pearls while doing housework? I don't think so

I certainly wasn't aware of it, and I know my parents were never asked about it. Apparently, I was part of a giant social test group. People around my age have unknowingly been studied for years to see what effect violence on television has had on society (I guess that's us).

Supposedly by the age of 12, a person will view something like 3,000-plus killings on TV. This study says that because of this, you can become desensitized and have a hard time separating fact from fantasy. This study even included cartoons – it seems even Bugs Bunny and Daffy Duck could have caused us physiological harm.

By the age of 6 or 7 even I knew those people who were shot on TV weren't really hurt or killed. The same "bad guy" that the Lone Ranger shot in a stagecoach holdup one week was "killed" by the Rifleman the next week for cattle rustling. Then just a few weeks later, the same guy was caught by Marshal Dillion for robbing the bank in Dodge City. I even saw him on trial for embezzlement that year on "Perry Mason." Even at that young age, I knew nobody was tough enough to survive all that.

I actually learned some valuable life lessons from cartoons. Yosemite Sam taught me to never put a lit stick of dynamite in my back pocket. In a way as powerful as anything I learned from Romper Room or Captain Kangaroo, Wile E. Coyote taught me to never run off the end of a railroad track to plunge into a 500-foot canyon. And just plain common sense, even at such a young age, told me that getting hit with a shovel did more to you than rearrange your nose like the bill on Daffy Duck. I won't even get into the Three Stooges. And they were around way before TV.

Some things on TV did confuse me and make me wonder, "Fact or fantasy?" I knew the "violence and mayhem" I saw wasn't real, but I wondered about Lucy and Ricky, Ward and June Cleaver and the Petries on "The Dick Van Dyke Show." I was always curious why they, and all the other married couples on TV, had separate beds. I wondered why my parents (and everyone else I knew) didn't, until I realized that it was like all the violence. It wasn't real either. I also never saw my mother, or any of my friends' moms, wearing a fancy dress, pearls and an apron while mixing up a cake when we came home from school.

It took me a little bit longer to come to grips with those things, but soon I knew they were also just fantasy. But, being really young, I had to confirm all this. I tried to order a safe from Acme Safe Co. to drop on my brother's head. When I found out Acme wasn't a real company, I was clear on fact and fantasy.

As far as becoming desensitized, after all these years of watching TV, I still know the violence is not real. But the cartoons are still real funny.

Bet you didn't know I hold a world record ...

I know a record should exist, but I couldn't find one. Nowhere in the books was there a record for dual running of the tenth of a mile; therefore I must be the only one who holds it.

I was raised on a berry farm. On rainy wintery days my older brother and I would usually work in the shop on equipment – trucks, tractors, etc. The shop was exactly one-tenth of a mile from our house. This equipment included school buses that we used to haul the pickers.

To complete the scenario, I've got to create the total picture. My brother has no hips to hold up his jeans, so when he squats down to work, he has an enormous amount of "plumber's cleavage."

Well, we were in the shop on a blustery cold and rainy day. I forget exactly what I was working on, but my brother was working on a bus's brakes, so he was squatted down. I had a full squirt oil can. When I saw him working, and I went by him with a fully primed oil can, something came over me.

I couldn't help myself. I backed up to make sure my aim was correct, then at a dead run, I took off and perfectly inserted the nozzle while squirting oil down my brother's pants.

You'd think my brother would see the natural fun and humor in the situation, but no – for some reason he got upset. Maybe it was that I surprised him and made him lose track of what he was doing. It couldn't have been all the oil I was able to squirt down his pants in good fun.

For whatever reason, he was mad. He immediately decided that he would respond by killing me. I couldn't understand why, but I could see that he was serious. I knew that I'd be better off by getting out of there as soon as possible.

The bus we were working on pretty near filled the shop, so it was difficult to get out of there quickly. I had to run around the bus a couple times, with my brother in hot pursuit as tools and small metal missiles (made of whatever was handy) flew toward me. While dodging those to preserve my life and avoiding getting caught and the certain pain that would result, I somehow got the door open. I took off for home at a dead run.

I knew that my mother would be there and could stop my brother from killing me, or at least from hurting me real bad. That knowledge, and the fact that my brother was still close behind me, made me cover that one-tenth of a mile in roughly 18 seconds.

There my fruitless search for some sort of record for posterity began. I know this record won't be duplicated and probably won't be beaten. Until it is, I know I am the champion, even if the event doesn't officially exist.

It shows that you don't need steroids or banned substances when running to break a record. You just need to avoid getting killed or injured. If only there was a safe way to make this event legal, and my form of performance enhancement a regular training method.

The bright side to all this? I know in my own mind that I probably hold a world record that will be as hard to duplicate as it is to prove.

A rose by any other name is still too hot

The sun was beating down, and it was HOT! Egg on the sidewalk kind of hot. I had just finished planting a large pine tree and was getting ready to shovel bark dust onto a slight bank covered with black plastic. I was sweating like a pack mule.

I had some high school kids helping me, and they were working fine despite the sweltering heat until someone said they heard on the radio that it was 102 degrees. Once they heard it was that hot, they dropped like flies. Even though it was my landscaping company and I was the boss, as I wiped the stinging sweat from my eyes I thought maybe there was something else I should be doing with my life.

I generally enjoyed landscaping and the feeling of creating something beautiful from nothing, but I couldn't help but wonder what my true aptitude was. Hopefully it would not be so reliant on the weather- hot and cold, wet or dry, etc.

At the local college there was a computer test designed by sociologists and psychiatrists. By using a complete personality and background analysis, the two-hour test, including hundreds of questions and statements, could make suggestions as to what your true aptitude might be. I was excited to see what the computer thought I should be. I spent a few hours in a cramped cubicle answering probing questions about myself, all to find traits that even I wasn't aware existed. The time came to finally push the final button and get the answer. I was excited!

I waited in anticipation to see if I was best suited to be a lawyer, teacher, scientist, or maybe a captain of industry. Finally, the computer produced the printout. My personality analysis showed that I was both creative and independent.

So far no surprises. It also said that I enjoyed solving obstacles and challenges. OK. Maybe this test had been a good idea.

This extensive psychological, computer-driven test revealed that I showed a strength toward "creating, enhancing, developing and constructing environmentally stable personal areas, creating pleasing surroundings through the use of natural materials, making a personal artistic statement based on the spatial placement of objects in said environment."

What?

After reading this several times, I realized what this meant was I showed a basic strength for... landscaping. And I'd thought I was just laying turf and planting trees. At least now I knew that I was already doing what I supposedly had a strength for.

From then on when I shoveled bark dust I realized that I was actually preparing the canvas of a "environmentally stabile personal space", and planting pine trees was making a "spatially relevant artistic statement." Somehow, knowing all this, I looked at what I did in a whole new light.

It was still really hot and I was sweating like a pack mule, but thanks to this science-based computerized test, I was sweating doing what I supposedly was meant to do.

For all that, it was still damned hot.

Fill 'er up, and don't look back

That '68 Toronado was some gas guzzler, but boy, was it cool and comfortable

I knew I had to do something. I was getting married, and we were going to drive to Los Angeles for our honeymoon. Back in 1973, gas was a major concern. At the time, the price was not the major concern; gas at any price was starting to get harder to find.

I had a 1968 Olds Toronado. It was a front-wheel-drive, luxurious car that handled like a custom roadster but had the ride and comfort of a Winnebago touring coach. It had power everything (even the radio antenna), climate control and retracting headlights. It also had the biggest engine you could get. It was an incredible car for a road trip.

It had one not-so-small problem though. It got only 10 miles per gallon on the highway, 10 in the city and what seemed to be about 8 sitting in the driveway. I knew with the threat of gas rationing becoming more and more likely and ever-rising prices, that this wasn't the car for our trip.

In what I thought to be a wise move considering the road trip, I sold my "dream car" and bought a Chevy Vega. Its total option list included a radio and heater that worked only when it wanted to (not very often). It had a stick shift, handled like a homemade go-cart and rode like a lawn tractor. I hit a cigarette butt once and it darn near threw me off the road. But it got 20-plus miles to the gallon, which made it a good road trip car.

The gas shortage became a reality on the first day of our honeymoon. We left on a Saturday and got stranded in Roseburg that night looking for an open gas station. I had to wait until Monday morning for one to open up. When it finally did, I filled not only the car, I also bought a 5-gallon can and filled it too. We were on our way!

We drove to San Francisco, checked into the hotel and went out touring the town. By the time we got back, my new wife was so sick I had to carry her into the room. The front desk called the paramedics.

While my wife was passed out and we were waiting for the paramedics, I read the paper and saw an article about the extreme danger of carrying a filled-gas can in an open car. Since our car was a hatchback coupe, it pretty much was exactly what the article was talking about.

The paramedics arrived, gave my wife some oxygen, and had us sleep with the windows open for the fresh air. Seems that she was overcome with all the gas fumes. Needless to say, I got rid of the gas can. The whole next day she was belching gas fumes. She smoked then but, because of the strong fumes, was deathly afraid to light up.

That all passed, and in spite of the car being pretty basic and kind of crude, the rest of the trip went well. Though the gas shortage did get worse, at least I had basic transportation that got decent mileage.

But as I was sitting in line on my designated day waiting to get my allotted 10 gallons of ever-more-precious fuel, I did a quick calculation.

My ultra-comfortable Toronado that I hastily got rid of got an average of 10 mpg and had a 20-gallon tank, making each tank last for 200 miles. The Vega I bought got 20 mpg and had a 10-gallon tank, making each tank last 200 miles. I was waiting in line for gas just as often, but not in the comfort I hastily gave up. Maybe I didn't think it through.

Sometimes hindsight can be really depressing.

It was a dark and stormy night (of course)

I had to go in and check it out – a whole super store dedicated to Halloween! Memories of candy corn, bobbing for apples and the adventure of trick-or-treating quickly came flooding back. When deciding to go as a cowboy, football player, or (for the girls) a princess or ballerina, was a socially and seemingly life-changing decision.

As I walked through the front door, I felt like I had entered a museum of the gross and macabre. Inside was a collection of ghoulish costumes, simulated bloody, dismembered body parts, an assortment of animated monsters and zombies.

Somehow the innocent festivities of kids looking forward to a pillowcase full of candy and the fun of dressing up in costumes, when about the scariest thing was a witch or a skeleton, had become more of a scary and grotesque time for adults. In fact, a billion-dollar one.

As I walked through the store, I saw some pretty cool stuff. But I also have to admit I was kind of grossed out, if not even spooked. It made my two adult costumes for parties look pale. One was the cowardly lion from "The Wizard of Oz." The other was as a convincing older woman- pretty scary and macabre, but for a whole different reason.

Then I saw the scene that made me realize I had to keep Halloween as innocent for the kids as I could.

It was a graveyard scene to put in your front yard, complete with headstones and an animated grim reaper. I didn't look at the cost because that scared me even more. Then I realized you could be truly spooked for free using only your imagination. It brought back a vivid memory.

It was a dark and blustery night (I think that's a law when telling a spooky story), and my brother and I were about 11 and 13. My parents were out for the evening at a meeting and thought we were old enough to stay by ourselves for a few hours. We were feeling pretty cocky and grown up.

After eating dinner and fighting about cleaning up, we settled down to watch TV. The rain was pounding against the large plate glass windows that were bowing inward as the seemingly gale force winds howled. Through all this, we thought we were too old for it to bother us.

Since we were home alone we felt old enough to do what we wanted, including stay up late. As the house creaked and settled in the blowing winds, we decided to watch "The Twilight Zone." No problem.

As the show played the mysterious theme music, we sat there, smug, ready to watch. The first scene was set in a small Southern town funeral home. There was a funeral going on with a closeup of a coffin, and the sad sounds of organ music. At about the time a particularly strong wind gust came, a grizzled hand started to slowly open the coffin from the inside!

We never did see what it was because in what must have been the speed of light, the TV was turned off and were in bed with our heads under the covers. We weren't scared, mind you. Just tired. After all, it was almost 9:30.

BOO! Look out – the tricks that your mind can play on you are no treat

You could tell it was October by the chill in the air. The leaves were starting to fall and change color, and it was getting dark earlier. We had just finished watching Disney's "Legend of Sleepy Hollow" and carved our Halloween pumpkins.

When I was little, the only thing that scared me more than the headless horseman were the flying monkeys in "The Wizard of Oz."

We cleaned up the pumpkin guts and carving residue. After putting them in some paper grocery bags, Mom asked me to take them out to the garbage. Our house sat on 5 acres, so our garbage cans were about 100 feet away from the house. It was behind a little wall that dad built so you really couldn't see it from anywhere.

I took the garbage and headed out. The full moon was peeking through the black misty clouds that were passing by. In the distance there was the lone barking of the neighbor's dog. The air was thick and foggy, a sign that autumn was here. It was just generally a spooky Halloween-time night.

I quickly headed to get rid of the garbage in the cans. I walked the 100 feet or so and put the garbage out. About that time, somewhere close by, I heard a cat screech and howl. That sent me back toward the house at more than a walk.

I started walking faster and faster. I had the eerie feeling that someone or something was behind me. All of a sudden, those 100 feet or so back to the house seemed more like half a mile. Before I knew it I was at a dead run.

I remember thinking of the quote I heard one time by Satchel Paige, the old baseball player. He said, "Don't look back, they may be gaining on you." I knew that if I looked back I would see a group of headless flying monkeys chasing me! So no way was I going to look back, and just the thought made me run faster and faster.

When I finally got to the back door, I could see the light from inside the house and feel the warmth of safety. I finally got in the back door, took a big breath, and sighed a sigh of relief. I knew I was finally safe from the combination of the two things I feared most.

Just as I caught my breath... WHAM! My big brother jumped out of the darkness of the laundry room next to the back door and grabbed me, yelling "GOTCH YA!"

I think at that tender age of 11 or 12, I had a cardiac event. I know that I had to change my underwear! It was right there and then that I realized I really don't like to be scared. To this day, I don't like horror movies, scary books or haunted houses (even for charity), and the thought of having to pay money to go see them has me really scared.

I guess I don't have to worry about reading anything from Stephen King, or seeing a movie about a headless flying monkey. I mean, come on, who would believe it anyway?

Oh, the wonder of the theater of the mind! Happy Halloween.

Cash flows in and out

We knew what it was even back then – we just didn't know it had a fancy name. We didn't know it was referred to as "cash flow." We just knew our cash had flowed somewhere. Back then when we were kids, we considered $5 to be a real stash of cash.

Since we lived in the country, we had a few different ways to make some money, but we were kind of excited when it was "Chittum bark" season. Chittum bark grows on birch-like trees in lower ground right at the edge of the woods or on uncleared ground, and there were a lot of these trees around. It was pretty easy to cut off pieces of the bark, and the general store a couple of miles away bought the bark by the pound and resold it to a company. We didn't know it then, but it's really Cascara bark, and it's used to make laxatives.

I say "general store" because it really was. You could do your grocery shopping, from bread and milk to peanut butter and everything in between. Then you could get fitted for a really good pair of boots and buy a pair of jeans. If you'd forgotten your anniversary, you could buy a fine box of chocolates and get a card. To finish clearing that last piece of ground, you could buy a case of dynamite. You could fill your truck with gas and help pay for it all with the money from the bark you just sold – kind of like a mini Wal-Mart, only 50-plus years ago. This store was run by only one man and his wife. It's not like it was really out in the country – it was only 6 miles from a good-size town and about 20 miles from a major metropolitan city. He was just a true merchant.

We went out and cut a couple of gunny sacks full of bark, took them up to the store to get them weighed, and then split up our few bucks.

The merchant posted the price – 38 cents a pound, for example. Not bad. We'd cut enough to make a couple bucks each. But that was for freshly cut bark. If it was dry, the price was 78 cents. Well, even if we were just 9 or 10 years old, we could see the dollar signs dance in our heads. We figured we'd take the bark back home and put it in our greenhouse to dry it and make the really big bucks.

While we waiting (for what seemed like forever) for the first load to dry out, we kept peeling more bark for some cash. The day finally came when the first bark we cut was what we thought to be dry enough. We excitedly put it on the general store's scale with visions of dollar signs in our heads, only to find out that the sacks each weighed about as much as a sack of hair. And not even wet hair at that. We must have let it dry too much. We collected about half of what we figured it would be and headed home, dejected.

By then the season was over with, and we learned one thing about "cash flow" – you had to put cash in before some could flow out. We weren't too comforted by the economics lesson we'd just learned. Oh well – we'd have to wait until next year to save any of the money to help future cash flow (like that was going to happen).

Even though entire classes and theories have been studied and debated, and even warrant a Nobel Prize, I learned the basic principle of "cash flow" without taking Economy 101. It really was all about a simple transaction and how it affected our cash supply: No cash flowing in, no cash flowing out.

And that's no Chittum.

CHAPTER 2
THE BEST TIME(S) OF YEAR

The shot heard 'round the block

The last hamburger and hotdog had been barbecued, the potato salad and watermelon were almost gone, and dusk was closing in.

It was our annual family Fourth of July celebration. And it had become an almost unspoken game of one-upmanship between us brothers-in-law as to who would have the most impressive (usually borderline illegal) fireworks display to shoot off at my father-in-law's cul-de-sac in Washington.

As usual, we were looking forward to the challenge.

As we gathered together our holiday displays, my father-in-law said, "Oh, by the way, a friend gave me this. It's a M-1000. It's supposed to be the equivalent to one-quarter of a stick of dynamite, so be careful."

This stick was about as big around as a paper towel roll, 2 inches long, with a short fuse. It looked like something straight out of a Bugs Bunny or Road Runner cartoon. It might've even been from the Acme Company. I think we all started to drool as we gently passed it around as though it were the Holy Grail. Compared to what *we* had, it kind of was.

We decided we couldn't set it off on the street pavement, so we would wait until dark and light it in a big field at a grade school about 8 blocks from the house.

Since it had a pretty short fuse, we had to figure out which one of us was going to light the stick. This was one time when walking with a cane came in handy for me – I didn't need some lame excuse as to why I wasn't up to the task. After someone else claimed to have a sprained ankle, a bad back, and so on, the youngest brother-in-law finally said he would. He always considered himself to be kind of a living action figure anyway, so we quickly said OK.

In the pitch dark, six of us climbed into a cargo van, headed to the school and parked by the big open field. The self-elected lighter took the valued cargo and disappeared from our sight. Soon we saw him emerge from the darkness at a full run. A few seconds later, we saw a bright flash. After a millisecond of what seemed like vacuumed silence, there was a loud concussion of an explosion. From a good 50 yards away we felt the ground shake, and the windows of the school even farther away rattled.

Now I would never condone doing something so flagrantly illegal, potentially so dangerous as to be life-threatening, against all common sense and just kind of overall stupid. But since we did it anyways, all I can say is we were lucky to not get caught, or worse, hurt. And also... it was GREAT!

We worried there might be police out looking for illegal fireworks, and if so, there was no way they could not have heard the explosion.

We all piled into the van and got away from there like a bunch of 12-year-olds afraid of getting caught with a Playboy and a pack of cigarettes. We drove straight into our father-in-law's garage and shut the door behind us.

We celebrated a few more Independence Days with the obligatory fireworks, but they seemed pale in comparison. After all our years of fireworks, we have never been able to match that.

I'm sure that if I were ever able to find another M-1000, it would bear this warning: "Use only under strict adult supervision, and keep out of reach of children, especially those 30-40."

Happy Fourth of July.

In search of the greatest fireworks ever

Never judge a book by its cover: I learned that lesson back when I was about 10. Basically, I learned never to base my opinion of the value of books, products, or even people, on their packaging, regardless of how drab or uninteresting. I trace this lesson and its usefulness back to one particular holiday.

It was almost the Fourth of July and as always, I was in search of the loudest, showiest, most awe-inspiring fireworks I could find. Somehow it seemed that it was my responsibility (I think I brought it on myself), and in looking back, I can easily figure out why.

Nothing can turn an otherwise responsible, mature, serious adult male of almost any age back into a 10-to-12 year old child faster than the chance to set off some good (possibly semi-illegal) explosions. And usually the higher the danger, the cooler. It must be a gender thing, because even my father would turn into a kid when we could obtain some good fireworks in a state where the ones that were illegal in Oregon were available. We always bought them when we could on our annual summer vacation to use on the next Fourth. They never made it past New Year's Eve.

With all of this in mind, I took my two nephews (who were 10 and 12) with me to continue the tradition of finding the ever-elusive "big bang" to cap off our annual July 4 celebration. We headed up north where the available legal fireworks were more varied. We kept our eyes peeled as we drove past the myriad of the countless stands. Suddenly there it was. A skyrocket the size of a large oatmeal box, stuck in the ground! I immediately planted my brakes and pulled in to inspect it. I don't know who was more excited, me or my young nephews.

It was called "The Big Bear." It looked fantastic, just like the ones in the Road Runner cartoons. It must be something great because it cost $50. Now all lessons learned, not to mention common sense, go out the window when it comes to potentially great, cool, and semi-dangerous fireworks. Of course I bought it.

My nephews and I envisioned this impressive rocket screaming across the sky in blazing glory, resulting in a fantastic peony-shaped explosion of colors and sounds. The closer to home we were, the more excited we got. This would be a great finale to the celebration.

When the barbecue was over and it grew dark, everyone there started to light the fireworks they had brought. There were some really great ones too. As it got close to the end, we were beside ourselves with excitement knowing we were about the light the greatest one ever!

Finally, it was our turn to amaze the crowd with our find. As my nephews stuck it in the ground and lit the fuse, the excitement built. We couldn't wait! They backed away and watched the fuse burn toward what was going to be an absolutely magical display!

With all eyes upon it, the burning fuse disappeared into the giant rocket. There was a sound equal to about three firecrackers twisted together, a puff of blue smoke, and kind of weak wheeze. Then it fell over. A sad and pathetic display.

The people to whom we had bragged about how great this pyrotechnic was going to be just thought it was a dud. They even seemed to feel bad for us. It was then that I realized that not judging something by its cover can work the other way too. Unfortunately, it cost me $50.

I can excuse that expensive lack of good sense. After all, it was potentially cool fireworks, and I know in the future I'll probably do it all again in search of the ultimate "big bang."

Some things are worth the risk

When I saw the little tents going up, I got a bit more excited than usual. They all said, "Fireworks for sale," but this was the first year that Washington allowed fireworks that were not legal in Oregon. Basically, that just meant more bang for your buck. The idea of having fireworks that were illegal in Oregon made me even more excited about the holiday.

The fact that we were going to have firecrackers and other things that would actually blow up was really cool to think about. Now remember I said there were legal only in Washington, and that meant that we had to smuggle them into Oregon. Knowing that this is going to happen, and that this is the first year, the media constantly warned about not taking illegal fireworks into Oregon.

Penalties could include a hefty fine, having your car impounded, and for really serious cases, even possible jail time. It supposedly would be a very serious deal to have these illegal fireworks in Oregon. Now all of these possible things that could happen made me and my brother-in-law even more curious as to what these illegal fireworks looked like. We had to see for ourselves.

We found an aluminum sided building with a large sign that said "Black Jack Fireworks." I went inside and looked around. Right in front of me were firecrackers, bottle rockets, skyrockets, aerial displays, ground displays and so much more! They had names like Black Sky Screamer, Missile Command Defense, The Battle of Gettysburg, North versus South, and all I had to do was pick them up and put them in my basket. I think I started to hyperventilate.

When I caught my breath and regained my senses, I started to throw the boxes into the basket. This was going to be a great Fourth of July!

Heading to the check stand, I began to think about all the different things that could happen if I were caught. I spent almost all of the money I had on fireworks. My car needed new tires and a tune-up, so I wouldn't mind if it was impounded. Since these were fireworks and thus all sense of good judgement goes out of your head – even if you are supposedly grown-up and respectable – I probably would risk jail time with a cellmate named Big Bubba.

When we left we drove around town, in case we were being followed by the police who might see our Oregon plates (see how the paranoia set in?), and even stopped and got something to eat. With our illegal stash hidden in the trunk the best we could, we thought it was about time to take a chance and head home.

We nervously headed to the interstate bridge. When we got to the Oregon border we thought we had it made. Just as I sighed a breath of relief, I looked in the rearview mirror and saw red flashing lights behind me. I had heard them term before but had never experienced flop sweat. We thought we'd been nailed for sure.

As the officer walked up to the window, I was already dripping wet, and probably looking really guilty about something.

The officer walked up to the window and said, "Sir, did you know your right taillight is out?"

I said, not trying to look guilty, "I didn't. I'll get it fixed right away. You never can be too careful, safety is always first."

I guiltily kept babbling on and on and on until my brother-in-law said, "We will get them fixed right away, officer," and with that the policeman walked back to his car.

It was then I realized I would not make a good criminal. If I got that nervous over a few firecrackers and a package of bottle rockets, I can only imagine how I would be with something *really* illegal.

It was well worth it. The fireworks were great. Somehow they seemed to be a little louder and brighter than usual. As it turned out, we would repeat the same thing for years. I would risk the heavy penalty of getting my car impounded or becoming prom queen of cell block 6! I mean, after all, we're talking really good, loud and dangerous fireworks.

I'm sure sometime in 1776 our founding fathers said, "Hey, some things are worth the risk."

A Fourth of July tip:
Make sure you know where the Roman candle is pointed

We would always celebrate the Fourth of July at my father-in-law's house. He lived in a cul-de-sac that seemed to be built for setting off a good selection of fireworks, both legal and somewhat illegal.

Now I was not allowed to light them, basically because even the "safest" ones all had the same warning on them: "Light and get away quickly!" I knew that was not going to happen, so I was relegated to orchestrating the festivities from the sidelines.

I realized this gave me a viewpoint to see all the colorful explosions and displays that were going on- not only ours, but the entire neighborhood's. We always looked forward to the Fourth, and it became almost a game as to who could "score" the best fireworks (meaning the most spectacular, therefore illegal) for the annual display.

This meant a lot of what we call aerials. The higher they would fly before blowing up in spectacular fashion, the better. But it also included some of the regular standbys like firecrackers, bottle rockets, and the ever-popular Roman candles. It was from my sideline position that I became way too intimate with a "safe" Roman candle.

For those of you who don't know, a Roman candle comes in a tube roughly an inch in diameter and a foot or so long. When lit, it shoots out colored balls. It is also safe to hold in our hands. There is a fuse on one end of the tube.

Having been around fireworks all my life, I got tired of just sitting on the sidelines and not getting to light anything. So one time I sat in my chair with a Roman candle held between my legs, pointed in front of me.

Now everyone knows that fireworks come out the end opposite the fuse. This is not the case with a Roman candle.

I lit the fuse between my legs, pointed the candle in front of me and waiting for the fun to start. And start it did. As I sat poised for fireworks entertainment, suddenly there were colorful, festive exploding balls of holiday fun shooting right into my crotch. I instinctively knew something was amiss!

Needless to say, I quickly corrected this error and carefully went on with the celebration.

The bright side to this? Never did a man who uses a cane or scooter for basic mobility get up and move so fast. I'd almost forgotten what it felt like to move that quick. The whole incident almost gave a new meaning to something "red, white and blue."

Mmm ... homemade for the holidays

When I walked in the front door, we were greeted by the warmth and sounds of a family holiday gathering. The table was already set. The turkey smelled great. I said hi to everyone and immediately headed for the kitchen to see how everything was going, and to offer my unasked-for help in sampling what I could.

After the requisite five or six times of being told to leave everything alone and to get out of there until dinner, I took the hint and did just that.

When dinner was finally ready, everyone sat down to a beautiful table. The turkey looked great, along with the bowl of mashed potatoes with the big chunk of butter on top. There was the dressing and the obligatory green bean casserole with the crispy onion topping (is that served any other time of year?), and a couple different kinds of vegetables along with assorted breads, rolls, and salads.

As I admired the bounty that was before me, I looked everywhere for my favorite holiday dish, thinking maybe it got left in the kitchen.

"Where are the candied yams?" I asked my sister, the main chef.

Her reply was one that took me a second or two to process: "I didn't make any."

It was like going over the river and through the woods to find out Grandma got run over by a reindeer.

After I got over the initial shock of not having a Thanksgiving dinner staple, I said quite indignantly, "You're kidding me!" - at which time I was told that if I wanted them so bad, next year I could make them. I said that was fine with me. After all, it couldn't be that tough.

I bought what looked to be perfect yams. I boiled and peeled, then cut them into pieces. I put butter and brown sugar on them, and adding my own touch, a few raisins. This sounds simple, but somehow there was stuff all over my kitchen – yam pieces, peels, butter, spatulas, knives, pans, sugar and other ingredients; it was a scene that resembled an Iron Chef war zone.

I put it in the oven for a while, then topped it with mini-marshmallows and browned them so they looked really good. All the mess and time was worth it because they turned out almost as good as Mom's.

A few days after Thanksgiving, Mom called me. "I hear you made the candied yams this year, and they were good," she said.

When I agreed they had turned out pretty good, but it wasn't the quick-and-easy dish it appeared to be, she said something that hit me like when I realized the truth about Santa: "Didn't you use the canned ones like I do?"

I wish she had told me earlier. But knowing the truth about Mom's candied yams didn't make them taste any different.

I guess it fits with the rest of the holiday dinner – the turkey that bastes itself and pops up a button to let you know when it's done; stove-top stuffing; gravy in a jar; cranberries shaped like a can; brown-and-serve rolls; pie bought at the bakery, topped with artificial whipped cream from a plastic tub. When you consider how good all this is, I guess candied yams from a can is no big thing. Besides, it's the people you're with and all the things you're thankful for that make the meal and time special.

You don't have to look very hard to find the bright sides around you. Be sure to thank the cook, and be careful what you say, or next time you might be making it yourself.

Turkey cooking 101: It can't be that hard... right?

It was our turn to host Thanksgiving and the turkey was my responsibility. I was going to make this one look like the one in the Norman Rockwell painting and be as moist as any that Grandma made. After all, mom and Grandma made it look easy. I was even looking forward to the challenge.

It couldn't be that hard.

First thing, I went out and purchased a 20-pound frozen turkey a few days before the holiday. I looked at it and thought there was no way it would thaw in time to cook it.

Now in doing what I thought was pretty quick and original thinking, I filled the bathtub with warm water and floated the frozen turkey in the tub (something I learned later you probably shouldn't do). My idea worked and by the next day, the turkey was ready to meet its fate.

So far, so good, and I was filled with confidence that this would be a simple task.

Now, I had never cooked a turkey before, so I relied on the directions I found in a cookbook.

First, wash the turkey after removing the bag inside. No problem. I placed it in the sink and gave it a good bath. Now it said to coat the turkey in oil or butter.

Wanting to make sure this turkey was good and moist, my best chef instincts told me to use both. So after slathering it with both until it was glimmering like a new penny, I was feeling cocky, thinking this really is easy. Then came the third step. It said to gently put the dressing into the turkey.

After I had already greased that bird so it was slicker than a sidewalk after a wicked winter ice storm, I found out there was no gentle way to add the dressing.

Every time I pushed the dressing in that slick bird would do its own private dance in the baking pan. I thought I would simply balance it with one hand while using the other to shove the dressing in. Should work fine... you'd think.

By about the third "gentle" shove, the greased bird slid out of the pan and right onto the floor. It skipped about three times, kind of like a stone on a flat pond. Because of the "five-second rule," I somehow was able to pick up the slick runaway bird and put it back into the baking pan. I added the rest of the dressing. Now I knew why they said gently.

With everything finally done, I put the bird in the oven. In the end, it turned out pretty good! After all, a turkey is "easy" to cook, or at least that's what I've been told.

I guess I'd already gained a false sense of confidence the day before when I made the candied yams. I boiled the orange spuds so I could cut them and arrange them into the large glass baking dish. I added the brown sugar and butter and baked them

29

in the oven, then topped it with marshmallows until they browned up to make a dish even Martha Stewart would approve of. I was pretty proud of my creation.

All I had to do was pop it in the microwave and heat it up for the big dinner.

When it came time to do just that, I realized the glass baking dish was way too large to *fit* into the microwave. So much for the way the dish looked.

I won't even talk about how you should always brown the bottom crust of a pumpkin pie.

All in all the dinner somehow turned out pretty good. Maybe it was all the family that was around or the realization of all that we had to be thankful for. Be more thankful for how easy Mom and Grandma DID make it look – and be thankful it's not your turn!

Happy Thanksgiving.

O Christmas tree - There's nothing like the real thing

We were getting closer and closer, and the excitement was building. We were going to Grandma's for Christmas like we had done every year. Along with Grandma and Grandpa, there was my aunt and uncle and cousin who lived a block away, as well as my great-grandparents and other relatives all in one area. It all made for an almost Currier and Ives family Christmas.

After the four or so hour drive, we were finally at our oh-so-familiar-yet-eagerly-awaited destination. I knew exactly what I had been looking forward to since last year.

The second I walked in the back door, I was enveloped in the warmth of those holiday smells of baking cookies, pumpkin pies, holiday candies, fudge and divinity, fir boughs and cinnamon-scented decorative pine cones. Grandma was also an Avon saleslady. I think she was her own best customer because the scent of her various creams, soaps, powders, and perfumes provided the subtle background. (To this day, sometimes a strong scent of Avon products can cause a holiday memory flashback.)

I was in holiday heaven. After I kissed Grandma, I headed into the front room to complete the Christmas magic. What I saw (and didn't see) stopped me dead in my tracks.

I looked all over for that beautiful green Christmas tree. It was not only the cap of all the decorations that created the whole season, but it also was the tree in every Christmas snapshot of my memory. It was the one I stood in front of with my Mickey Mouse guitar that Santa gave me. It was there on Christmas morning when we all ran downstairs to see how good Santa thought we were. It was there in the background as we watched the Lawrence Welk Christmas show every year. As I looked everywhere, it was not to be found.

Instead, over in the corner was a 4-foot aluminum, silver and shiny tree shaped object that was on a revolving stand. It didn't have a single ornament on it, but it was accompanied by a large color wheel that made the silver thing appear to constantly change color. Even though it was kind of pretty in its own way, it radiated all the holiday warmth of the lobby of a savings and loan branch office.

I guess since I was the youngest grandchild, and old enough that Santa wasn't coming to see me anymore, Grandma and Grandpa thought they didn't need a real tree anymore either (or the hassle and the mess.)

It was Christmas, after all, and the missing tree didn't totally dampen the true holiday warmth and celebration, but it did have a subconscious impact on me. After a few Christmases without a real tree, we stopped going there when my older sister brought her new baby home to our house for the holidays, and I became responsible for getting our tree.

That 4-foot, cold, and un-festive "tree" seemed to affect me. I went the opposite way. I always made sure that our tree was not only real, but also larger than it really should have been. My theory: If having a tree for two of the 52 weeks of the year meant you had to sacrifice a little furniture to make room for it, so what? I tended to overcompensate by making sure that the tree was the focal point of the entire season. I guess in a psychiatrist's view I suffered from a case of "tree envy".

To this day, I always have not only a larger tree than the house calls for, but one that has enough lights, garland and different ornaments that it looks like it could be in a Norman Rockwell painting. This doesn't mean that simple aluminum "tree," or any other kind of tree regardless of size, color, or type (real or not), is not someone else's important tradition. It's just not my own.

With all that said, I guess I'll sit here and look at my tree and hope that PBS plays a rerun of a Lawrence Welk Christmas show while I sing along with my Mickey Mouse guitar.

The prettiest tree of all

I'm really picky about my Christmas trees, and this year was no different than the others. As I drove around looking for a good noble spruce, I found it hard to be jolly when I saw the prices.

The cheapest one I found that I would be pleased with was going to cost at least $40. Now I'm not cheap or anything, especially when it comes to Christmas decorations, but 40 bucks? And it's only going to be up for about two weeks.

Since we owned a nursery, my dad couldn't understand why we would pay for a tee when we could just get one of ours. When I explained that we didn't raise the right kind, he always acted upset. But he must not have been because he was always excited to get it.

Our house had high ceilings, and I always got a big tree. My brother had a great idea to save the money that he truly thought was a waste: he and a friend would go up to Mount Hood and cut one.

In preparation for this, knowing he would come home with a big tree, we moved all the furniture out of the way and brought the decorations up from the basement. Dad stoked the fire while Mom passed around the hot chocolate. We made popcorn chains. It was just like "The Waltons." We sat in this Norman Rockwell pose waiting for my brother to come home with a big freshly cut tree to complete the picture.

We waited... and waited... and waited. Finally, we heard the truck pull up. I was getting excited in anticipation.

My brother stormed in. His face was red. The first thing he said was, "Don't say a damn thing." (Never heard John Boy say that.)

It didn't take long to see what happened. He went outside and came back in with a sorry, scrawny half-yellow and short tree. It was really sad. I think it was the tree that Charlie Brown thought wasn't good enough.

Dad took one look at it and laughed under his breath. "Don't worry," he said. "We can fix this up."

He went downstairs and got the drill. We clipped and rearranged the limbs from the fuller side to the thinner side. Dad drilled holes in the trunk of the sad tree, and we filled in the bare spots.

When we were done, we had a decent-looking tree. When we got it all decorated, it looked really nice. Dad stood back and said, "That's the prettiest tree we've ever had".

Even if he said that every year, it really was one of the prettiest trees, at least as I remember it. I think it was because the tree looked so sad at the start, and the whole family had fun working together to turn it into a truly beautiful symbol of the holiday season.

Remembering all this, I went back and spent $40 on a tree. When that tree was up and decorated, I truly think it was the prettiest tree we ever had.

Happy holidays from "The Bright Side."

O Christmas Tree

Make mine a wooden one, bare spots and all

It was pouring down rain, cold and windy. It was the only weekend when I could get my Christmas tree, and the weather wasn't cooperating. This made me think about something I swore I would never do. I thought about getting an artificial tree.

Now I've always been a real traditionalist and taken a lot of pride in my trees. For me it was always the bigger the better. There are 52 weeks in a year, and I always had the idea that you could have furniture in your house for 50 weeks and have a tree for two.

My favorite tree measured 17 feet from side to side. When people asked me where I put it, I just said "In the house." When pressed farther as to where in the house, all I could say was, "In the house." It was so misshapen on one side that it had room for a small toy train set. The thought of a perfectly shaped artificial tree was hard for me to grasp. So I listed all the pros and cons.

First of all, I could put up the tree day or night, and didn't have to rely on the weather to get it out of the closet. I could put away the chain saw, hammers, plywood stand and cable guide wires to put it up. No more mud and dirt from dragging it from the rainy outside through the house. No more having to worry about finding a truck to haul the tree. No more having to keep it watered so it would stay fresh.

This was such a big step for me to give up a closely held tradition, I took a friend with me to make sure that I bought the most realistic looking "fake" tree I could find. We finally picked one, and by going over all the pros, I justified the $125-plus price tag and bought it.

Excited about starting a new tradition, I put up my new tree. It wasn't as quick and easy as I thought it would be, but not bad. At least I didn't have to worry about rigging up some sort of stand. (My other trees were always too big for regular stands.) After I put all the lights and ornaments on, I stood back and really looked at it with a different eye.

It was really pretty and festive. I thought it was a beautiful and cheery tree – if it was in a bank lobby. After I had done the best I could, I realized that the tree was too perfect. It had no personality and would basically look the same year after year, ornament placement and all.

I soon realized that I missed going out in the chilly, wet weather on the hunt for a tree. I missed getting the truck and chainsaw and building the stand. I missed finding a tree with some "personality." I missed turning the tree to find the best side, and I missed figuring out which ornament best fills any holes that are there.

As I studied my $125-plus "convenience," I realized that as festive as that overly perfect tree was, it was indeed artificial. It looked more like something I took out of my Christmas decorations box, blown up and put in the corner.

That year was the most expensive tree I ever had, because I promptly gave it away when the season was over. One year was enough. Back to the good old messy days of cutting down and decorating a real tree, warts, hassle and all. While an artificial tree works for some, not me, thank you.

Merry Christmas!

P.S. Does anyone have any hints on getting pitch out of carpets?

Hot cocoa and chainsaws? Must be Christmas

We rounded the corner and there it was, standing among all the others and looking like something straight out of a Christmas card. We'd found the perfect tree. We couldn't believe our luck – it was the right height and everything.

As we got ready to cut it, I realized it was a green spruce. That meant not only did it have really sticky needles, but you should wear those thick leather welder's gloves to handle it. However, thinking about how great it would look, we found back the pitch and irritation that even getting close to it caused. It was almost like those needles protected it like the quills of a porcupine.

When we got the tree home, somehow it had suddenly grown a whole bunch since it was in the field. Green spruce aren't as flexible as other varieties. When they are 5 feet wide, they're really hard to cram through a 3-foot door. With a lot of help, we got it inside – and after all that, found out it was about a foot too tall.

I wasn't about to cut my arms and hands by using a handsaw to cut a foot off the bottom, so I went out to the garage and got my chainsaw. When I fired it up, it belched out a kind of pretty blue smoke as I cut through that tree quicker than you can say "fruitcake," (which you know someone will give you). When I was done, the smoke hung around the ceiling, adding to the holiday atmosphere.

I put on my thick canvas work coat and a good pair of gloves and with the help of some friends, got the tree to stand up. Then the real holiday fun could start! We got all the lights and decorations ready and then sat back to plan our attack. First we strung the lights. We decided that maybe the pain and hassles we suffered fighting that tree might be worth it after all. It could be the almost perfect tree.

But before the lights were finished, the hot cocoa with marshmallows had turned into hot buttered rum (really light on the butter). The traditional Christmas carols had turned into something else (a piece of Christmas trivia: very few swear words rhyme with holly, jolly, or even snow). We did discover one good thing about the tree, however. After trying one time, the cat wouldn't come near it.

After a few long and painstaking hours, we were done with the tree. All the pain, pitch, rashes, cussing and fighting was almost worth it. It was beautiful. Not only did we have a Christmas-card worthy tree, we had developed a new holiday scent: chainsaw exhaust and skin rash antiseptic. I'm not sure why, but for some reason it just didn't catch on. That was alright, after a couple of days it faded away.

All said and done, it was well worth the effort. As long as we didn't think about taking down the tree, we totally enjoyed the season.

Would we do it all again? Probably not. But happy holidays anyways.

That warm gladness you feel might come from giving to others

It was more than the brisk chill in the air, or the smell of evergreens and fir boughs, or even the brightly lit storefronts, houses and malls. What really made me realize the Christmas season was in full swing was the warming sound of the ringing bells at the Salvation Army's red kettles. Somehow those little bells cut through the din of traffic to create a seasonal sound as welcoming as a warm fire on a snowy day.

Even when I was little, I always made sure I had some change handy so I could "feed" the kettle whenever I passed one. That's probably why, when I got older, I readily volunteered to ring the bell myself through my Kiwanis Club in support the Salvation Army. As the years went by, I became chairman of that endeavor. Even though it didn't make any actual money for the club itself, it was by far my favorite project.

I found out that by adding some live Christmas music, we drew more attention and as a result raised more money. What started out as a sax quartet over the years became a full seven-piece brass choir. As chairman, I was responsible for scheduling the members.

Because our club was always a top money raiser, we were given a prime, inside, high-traffic spot. On what became our best money-raising day, I scheduled myself in my electric wheelchair on one side and Father Vic, an Episcopalian priest, on the other, with the kettle and music just past us at the end. Since the shoppers had to walk through us on their way into the store, I had inadvertently created a "gauntlet of giving." When people passed by, they heard the music first, saw me in a wheelchair second, a priest third, and then the kettle. For whatever the reason (guilt, shame, or just the overwhelming spirit of the season), the money really flowed. I even got a thank you card from the Salvation Army for our efforts.

All this confirmed that the saying "It's better to give than to receive" not only is true, it also proved to me that by giving – your money, time, etc. – you receive even more. When you think that the few coins you put in the kettle could make Christmas dinner possible for a single mother and her kids or help pay the power bill for the family of a man who was out of work, the feeling you receive is more rewarding that the amount you gave.

So take a name off a giving tree, help pack some food boxes, donate some warm clothes to a mission. It's OK to be selfish and receive as much as you can by giving even more – whether in the spirit of The Little Drummer Boy or the largesse of a reformed Ebenezer Scrooge on Christmas Day.

Happy holidays and Merry Christmas from the Bright Side!

CHAPTER 3
DOLLARS AND SENSE

You have entered 'The Retail Zone'

I seemed like a normal, beautiful summer day. It was July 25th, to be exact. I still had a little irritation from the burn I got from lighting fireworks.

I went shopping for some ointment for my still somewhat-fresh holiday burn. I went to that drugstore that seems to be on every other corner – the combination pharmacy/grocery/photo/ electronic/candy and cosmetics/limited home hardware/office supply/small electric kitchen appliances and more store. While you're waiting for your prescription, you can get a Slurpee or a passport picture taken.

All I wanted was a small tube of ointment. Little did I know that I was entering "The Twilight Zone."

I went directly to the back of the store to get what I was looking for. I found it, and on my way up toward the cashier I went down the "Back to School" aisle. I looked at the date and realized that kids had been out of school less than two months, but according to the store it was soon time to go back. When I looked at the notebooks, paper, crayons, and backpacks, I noticed it was all priced and marked with such a sense of urgency that you'd believe school was going to start next Monday.

Still shaking my head at how early it seemed to be talking about going back to school, I went to the next aisle and ran into a sight that stopped me in my tracks: a display of pumpkins, fall scarecrows, and decorations reminding me to "Give Thanks".

I had been in the store only 15 minutes, had gone about 150 feet and covered 3 aisles – and four months had flown by. I didn't know whether I had been stopped while time went on, or if time was being compressed and taking me with it. Either way, I decided I'd better get out of there. I was aging too fast already.

I was afraid to go down another aisle. I didn't want to see what possible surprise would be there, or how much more time would zip by. I looked straight ahead and went to check out. I quickly got back outside and was greeted by the warmth of the midsummer sun.

Realizing that I was back to where time was supposed to be, I concluded that if this wasn't a "Twilight Zone" parallel universe, then I had just entered "The Retail Zone." Apparently, that zone had a calendar and sense of time all its own. If it can be November when it's only July in our zone, after Christmas flies by it will be time for Easter. Too early, you say? Not in "The Retail Zone!"

I can't think of any other reason why we see all these seasonal trappings for three or four months at a time. When the real holiday arrives, the music of each season has already been on the radio for over a month. In "The Retail Zone," there's nothing that makes the actual holiday itself special.

That's my explanation for this phenomenon – although it makes me wonder about that one guy in the neighborhood who never takes his Christmas lights down. He just unplugs them. Maybe he knows something I don't.

But wait! There's more!

It was almost too good to resist. For just shipping and handling charges, I could get a second one free! I hadn't even thought of buying one, but when I saw on TV how much I really needed a PedEgg to get rid of all that thick calloused skin on my feet, the idea of getting two for the price of one was the clincher.

The price for the first one was $10 plus a $7.98 shipping and handling charge; a grand total of $17.98. Add my shipping and handling for the free one, and my total was $25.96! I thought it was free.

I soon found out you can use only one at a time.

How much handling can something the size of an egg in a box take? Oh well. I should have learned when I ordered that pen developed by NASA that could write upside down and under water. I don't know if it could really do that, because I realized that I seldom write upside down, and never under water (at least not on purpose). That cost $5.98 to handle.

When I saw the Perfect Pancake, though, I knew I could use it. But wait, there's more! A lot of cool things came with it, like heart-shaped inserts to make heart pancakes (a $20 value – where would I buy them by themselves?) I got everything that was promised, and I couldn't wait to try it out.

After I mixed up the batter, I made my first pancake. It worked like a charm. I had a perfect pancake. One. I soon realized that by the time I had made a really good stack, the first pancake was cold.

Besides, I had to clean up all that batter I'd made by following a recipe in the free cookbook. I forget how much the shipping and handling charges were for this future garage sale item, but I know it was quite a bit more than the item itself.

Recently I saw another offer on TV that caught my interest. It was a Chia Pet shaped like President Obama. As always, there was an assortment of "But wait! There's more!" offers that went along with it. I couldn't see it as anything but tacky. Somehow, the plight of black Americans from dire slavery through segregation and racism to achieving the highest office in the land seemed to warrant much more than just a throwaway Chia Pet.

Then I received a Chia Pet (mistakenly, I'm sure) in a white elephant gift exchange. It wasn't as cheesy-looking as I thought it might be. I put it in my special place of honor, clearing a space on my fake mantel over my fake fireplace. It sat between my painting of Elvis on velvet that I got in Tijuana (the only place I've seen that art form practiced) and my picture of four dogs playing poker (a find I was lucky enough to stumble across at a garage sale). When I looked at it, my heart swelled with patriotic pride.

Tacky? I think not. But wait! There's really more? I don't possibly see how that can be.

Double your money: Fold it in half, put it in your wallet

It was kind of a relief. This could be the way to really help finance my daughter's college education. Even though I felt like it was insider trading, or at least something that you might get investigated for, I figured I'd try it. How can you get in trouble when you really have no idea about the world of high finance?

I had a good friend who was a successful sheetrock contractor. He told me that the company – the largest wallboard manufacturer in the world – was fighting a hostile takeover and its stock price had dropped to $1 per share. He told me the price of this stock had been as high as $80 per share but dropped to avoid the takeover. It has been on the Dow Jones board for almost 100 years, so it was no fly-by-night company. He then told me that it was a sure thing, and I should do what I could to buy stock in it.

Since I respected his business success, I did just that. With $100 and a call to my aunts' broker, I plunged into the world of high finance. In my eye, I had become a player in the market.

Now I found myself reading the financial page of the paper every day to check on my "sure thing" entry into what I thought would be the successful and profitable world of wheeling and dealing. I was now part of that bastion of capitalism- the stock market! I just knew that this small (yet pretty big to me) investment was going to grow. I envisioned that someday I would be like the guy in the old movies with a phone in each hand yelling "buy" in one and "sell" in the other.

I looked at my stock's progress every day. Every day the stock price just sat there, never changing by more than half a point at a time. After a month or so of looking every day, I looked at the price only if the paper happened to fall open to the financial page. I was starting to get depressed and bored with my "sure thing." My visions of being an investment wizard were starting to fade.

My total stake in the world of the global economy had grown from $100 to the staggering figure of $116. I started to realize that maybe this investment wasn't all I thought when I found out that after the commission to sell it was paid to the broker, I would have LOST money.

Just when I had come to the conclusion that I probably should write off my "investment" and stop dreaming of being the next Warren Buffett, I got a letter from the company that I'd tied my money up in. As I started to read the letter, the first words I saw were "stock split." I got so excited that all the feelings I had of being an investment mogul started up again. My 100 shares had grown!

With my smug feelings reinstated, I kept reading the letter, and those smug feelings left quicker than they'd returned. It seems that there had been a REVERSE stock split. I would be issued one new share for every 50 shares I held. I now owned only two shares of the floundering company instead of 100. On top of that, the value of the new shares totaled $84. My "sure thing" that I thought might help pay for college would soon barely be enough for postage to send away for some trade school brochures.

I guess I don't have the patience or stress level to involve myself in the world of Wall Street. Especially when I really had no idea what I was doing. I'd better leave it to the pros. Maybe someday I might have the guts to invest in some conservative mutual funds.

In the meantime, I think I'll follow my great-uncle's advice. The only "sure way" to double your money is to fold it up and quickly put it back in your wallet. I found that it doesn't grow much, but at least it doesn't do many reverse splits.

The 'curse' of the one-eyed car

I have been no stranger to unplanned vehicular mishaps. After totaling several cars in a three- or four-year period (believe it or not, they were not my fault), and being run into or driven off the road by people with no insurance, I began to think I had a target on my car.

Even though I knew that probably wasn't true, I made sure to keep up on my insurance so if someone with no insurance ruined or wrecked my car, I wouldn't be left without wheels.

Then a few years went by, and my car and driving record went relatively unscathed. Maybe my imagined curse had finally run its course. I decided it was time to get a car that merited more than minimum liability only. I bought a car that was only a few years old, and I was proud to drive it. I didn't even look the other way when someone asked, "Whose car is that?"

I washed the car every week and kept the interior spotless. I also enjoyed not being nickeled and dimed to death by constant car repairs. Safety and passing emissions tests were no longer major concerns.

I noticed that one of the headlight lenses was cracked. The slightly broken glass had allowed some water to seep into the housing. I thought I could just replace it with a new glass lens. No big deal, or so I thought.

I found out the entire headlight housing unit had to be replaced. A new unit was about $250. Ouch! After searching for a used one, I found a unit at a wrecking yard- it was still $140! I finally had a decent car that I was proud of, so I bit the bullet (really hard), paid the money and got the light fixed. It looked really good.

A couple of weeks later, I was driving home from work with a new sense of being "curse free." A pickup on my left ran a stop sign and proceeded to pull out in front of me. Mayhem ensued. I pretty much ran into the truck, smashed up the front of my car and vaulted about 100 yards into a tree in someone's front yard.

In a real switch, the other guy had insurance! My brief ER stay and ambulance ride, along with my totaled car, were all covered!

I didn't see my totaled car until I went to the wrecking yard where it had been towed. My once proud, fully insured vehicle was now a sad shell of mashed, twisted metal and chrome parts.

In fact, I noticed that every recognizable part of the front of my car had been smashed and violently assaulted except one. The headlight that I'd just paid $140 for was completely untouched and in one piece.

It was just staring at me as though it were saying, "Don't get too cocky," or it was giving me the stink eye as if to warn me, "Just wait, there's more!"

Try as hard as I might, I can't really find a good way to spin this story, except to say it shed a whole new light (pardon the pun) on my views of insurance, curses, bad luck etc.

But most of all, I was left with the thought that maybe my own driving actually might be to blame. Either way, I couldn't help by feel I was being watched.

The 1 cent check

I was pretty excited when I got a letter in the mail the other day. I could see by the window in the envelope that it contained a check! Since I wasn't expecting a check, and I didn't know who it was from, my curiosity added to my excitement.

I hurriedly opened this surprise and found a check for – 1 cent. One penny. Now I've never seen a check for 1 cent before, and I looked at it closer to see if it was a joke or something.

It was from the Medicare Secondary Payment Recovery Contractor. It was in reference to a Medicaid demand overpayment to some beneficiary.

Huh? I still had no idea what the heck it could be about, but I also practiced the old motto of "Never look a gift horse in the mouth." I didn't know whether to cash it or frame it as a conversation piece.

One thing it did, though, was to give me a whole new respect for the lowly penny. Seeing it in the form of a genuine bank check made me realize it did have real value. Maybe I could start a portfolio of so called "penny stocks." Who knows where this might end?

I realized its value even more when I figured how much it probably cost to issue this 1 cent check. First of all, the postage to send it was 46 cents. The check itself was printed on "chemically reactive paper that includes a tamper evident chemical wash warning box." Again, huh?

Comparing that to what my simple, plain, mail-order checks cost me, this high-tech check must have cost at least 25 cents.

Then there's the cost of the envelope (maybe 2 cents), the time of the staff to put it all together, the actual printing of the check and the computer system it takes to monitor it all, and so on and so on... Let's just say a total of 50 cents more. So far this check cost than $1.25. For a 1 cent reimbursement!

All this makes me look with a little more respect at that small cottage cheese cup full of pennies I have stashed in my sock drawer. To paraphrase an old saying... a penny saved is $1.25 earned.

Hey, this costs only a dollar! *
(* he said, $48 later)

When they couldn't make a clean, even cut on the thin wrapping paper I was trying to use, I knew it was time to break down and buy a new pair of scissors. Since I rarely use them, I decided I wasn't going to spend any more than I had to. (Plus, I've been told I'm sort of cheap.)

With that in mind, I went to the Dollar Store to buy a $1 pair of utility scissors. The whole concept of the Dollar Store always mystified me. I just couldn't figure out how they could make any money a buck at a time. I took my dollar with me thinking I was going to get a good pair of utility scissors for just a single buck! I was ready.

When I walked in the store I saw the housewares were at the back. As I headed in, I quickly learned that the profitability of these stores is based the magic of THE IMPULSE BUY!

Before I was in there five minutes, I was already over my planned one dollar. I saw an eight pack of AAA batteries for $1! I wasn't even sure I really had any devices that needed AAA batteries, but it was such a great deal. THEY'RE ONLY A BUCK, I thought as I tossed them in the basket.

I headed toward the scissors but kept running into things that I had no idea I needed. I put them in my cart with one thought going through my head: IT'S ONLY A BUCK!

Before I knew it, I had a pack of light bulbs, a pair of pliers, a claw hammer, some shampoo, food containers (I don't even cook for myself, which I also should have remembered when I threw in that 10-inch nonstick frying pan), and a whole bunch of other important things.

The basic cheapskate in me just couldn't pass up deals like these. Then I wandered into the candy and food section. I saw candy that I hadn't seen for years, so before I knew it I had some different licorice, candy bars and long-forgotten cookies in my cart, all the time thinking, IT'S ONLY A BUCK!

After I had to transfer my hand basket to the large rolling shopping basket, I was done. I went to check out, feeling pretty cocky about all the great deals I made that were ONLY A BUCK!

When the checker was done with my "cheap stash," the total was $48! She then reassured me of what a great assortment I had for such a low price. Somehow, I was not comforted by it. I had just spent $48 at the Dollar Store.

When I got home and put everything away, I realized somewhere between the excitement of the cheap shampoo and the unneeded frying pan, I had forgotten to even get the $1 scissors that I went for in the first place.

I decided I had to go to a regular store and bite the bullet, spend the 6 or 8 bucks or more and just buy some scissors. I decided that I couldn't afford to go back to the Dollar Store to get another $48 pair of scissors. Besides, the frying pan filled the drawer I was going to keep them in anyways.

Missed Opportunities

It sounded like fun. Looking at cool cars that had been restored brought me back to my "good old days". As I walked through the first of many cruise-ins of the summer, I realized two things. First the cars WERE really cool. They were the cars that I wish I had when I was in High School. But I also realized something else. In the years that followed, it seemed like at one point or another, I owned many of these cars. Except, I don't remember them being this cool at the time. Sure they were pretty nice when I had them, but they didn't seem to draw the crowds of onlookers and their comments that these cars do now.

I realized what an investment opportunity I had passed up and without even knowing. My first car was a 1963 Chevy Impala Super Sport. It was white with a red and chrome interior with bucket seats. It was (as was said then) "really fine". I paid a grand total of $750 for it, but back then that was about the same as book value. I saw three different '63 Chevy's. The best one was also for sale. It wasn't nearly as nice as the one I had, so I asked what he wanted for it. He said $ 11,000! When I showed some disbelief at that price, he told me it was worth at least that.

That really depressed me. I figured out if I had kept my car, my investment would have increased in value like a gazillion percent! Definitely more than the 3.4% that my CD is earning. When he asked what I did with mine, I got even more depressed. I told him that I traded it in for a '68 Toranado. He said "Let's see, I see 3 cars like yours here in this cruise in of classics, but not a single Toranado. How smart a move was that?" When I realized he was right, I had no comeback. For some reason, it was hard, really hard, to enjoy the rest of the cars- probably because that one incident just reminded me of all the other chances I missed to make some good investment choices. Like the new house I should have bought for $19,000. Or the bank I could have bought some stock in. It's only increased about 500%... no reason to bore you with all the rest.

The reason I'm telling you all this is to make everyone feel better about all their bad choices or missed opportunities. You're not alone! There, I've done my job. With that in mind, knowing you're going to be careful not to miss another "sure thing", I have a timeshare opportunity available for the meager investment of only $1,000! Don't let another opportunity pass you up. This will not only make an excellent return on your investment (almost guaranteed), but it will save you from definite depression later when thinking about what a good investment you didn't pass up. For just a small amount of $100 (only to show your sincerity) I'll send you the details. (P.S., as with any investment, there's a small, but very small chance that returns won't happen.)

Don't let another almost surefire chance pass you by! You may be sorry later. If you don't fall for, I mean take advantage of, this excellent chance, you can't take advantage of the easy returns. I know I can't.

CHAPTER 4
LIFE LESSONS

Learned or not!

Oh, those seductive Black Vines

I turned the drawer upside down and went through everything in it. When I desperately tore up my "stash" spot in search of one last piece, I knew I had hit rock bottom. I needed help to end this terrible addiction. It had started to take control of my life.

It all started innocently enough. During a simple trip to the grocery store, between picking up my regular bagels and making my way over to my weekly bananas and oranges, there it was. Black licorice on sale. Half price! And not just the regular box of vines, but the jumbo bag! They were fresh and soft, I couldn't resist.

Now I like to think I can spot a bargain when I see one, so I threw it in my basket of otherwise pretty healthy stuff. I didn't even give it a second thought except feeling proud of my wise find.

I got home and started putting my groceries away. The last thing was this jumbo bag of incredibly fresh and soft black licorice. Even though it was probably too close to dinner, I thought a couple of pieces wouldn't hurt. I tore the corner of the bag open and took out a couple of vines.

When I finished with those, I took out a couple more, and then a couple more. Then I started taking three at a time. Before I knew it, about a quarter of the bag was gone. I knew then that I was in trouble. I tried to justify it by thinking, "Hey, its fat free" (so is a 5-pound bag of sugar and a spoon).

I really knew it was a problem when I told my friends how great a deal it was and gave them some licorice. Before I knew it, they were also hooked on this legal confectionary. It made my own addiction seem OK if I could share it. Pretty stupid, I admit, but somehow that soft, fresh black licorice had me in its control. I knew I had to stop the madness.

Knowing I couldn't do it by myself, I figured there might be some sort of 12-step group I could join, or at least maybe a support group.

In investigating, I found groups for alcoholics, gamblers, sex addicts, wife abusers, compulsive shoppers, credit card abusers, overeaters, under-eaters, hoarders, plastic surgery addicts and forms of compulsive behavior that I didn't know even existed. My exhaustive research didn't turn up anything even barely related to the evils and easy seduction of those seemingly innocent black vines.

As a last resort, I called some private rehab companies. You know, the ones that advertise on TV, the ones that make curing a helpless addiction sound like a pleasant stroll in a nice country meadow. I related my whole sordid story.

After being hung up on and laughed at countless times, one counselor finally listened. Thinking maybe I was finally going to get some help, she said, "Wow, it was how cheap? Where did you get it?"

I could tell by the genuine excitement in her voice that not only was I not going to get any help, but I had brought one more person to the "dark side."

I made up my mind that I was going to take control over a simple children's candy, but the next time I went to the store I was still drawn to the candy aisle. There it was, but... my addiction was cured! All my worrying came to a sudden stop. The licorice was not on sale anymore!

The price tag was double what it was when I bought that first bag and started my downward spiral into a dark hole. All it took was the price of $1.50 more per bag. What a relief.

For once, my habit of being value conscious (or outright cheap) finally paid off. I no longer had a monkey on my back. That monkey had started to do the river dance on my shoulders.

With the problem caused and solved by a change in prices, I got nervous when I saw a really good sale on Skittles.

"Not again," I said to myself.

I went back to the produce section as quickly as I could and bought more bananas than usual.

Now if Peanut M&Ms go on sale...

It all started all so innocently ...

"Every time a door shuts, another opens." That's a good inspirational piece of advice, which usually works out. But there is another saying: "What goes up must come down." It seems that both can work for and against each other. Every time I close the door on one addiction or compulsive behavior, a door to another one seems to indeed open, and a downhill descent almost always comes with it.

In the past, I've successfully lost 100 pounds, quit smoking after 19 years, stopped chewing my nails, got over my addiction to black licorice (still a work in progress) and overcame many obsessive traits that weren't healthy. It seems that every time I shut the door on one thing, sure enough, another one opened – one time really wide.

A Facebook friend asked me to play him in a simple little game called "Words with Friends." Little did I know that I was starting the equivalent of computer crack cocaine. Just one little game, and I was hooked. Before I knew it, I was simultaneously playing 11 games with five different people. Every time I quit playing to do something else, I felt guilty. I felt I was being rude to the people I was playing, as if they were just sitting there waiting breathlessly for my next move.

What started as an innocent way to play a game with friends had become a problem when I realized that I had spent three hours one morning playing non-stop. The only reason I stopped then was because I was waiting for one of the five or six others to make their move. While waiting, I saw that I had been invited by "friends" to explore a game called "Farmville." I could build up my "farm" by adding animals, plants, buildings and such.

Then there was "Bubble Safari," "Lucky Slots," "Mafia Wars" and more all competing for what could be constructive time spent. They seem like they're some pyramid scheme because the success of these games rely on getting as many people involved as possible.

When I first bought a computer, I was excited about all the possibilities it would provide. I could do my taxes, organize all my expenses, create correspondence both business and personal. Keep important records that I could retrieve at any time, research things through the Internet and make instant contact with others worldwide. The possibilities were endless!

Then I was lured into the world of computer-game addiction, and apparently I wasn't alone. I felt like someone who had a microwave oven and only used it to boil water or make popcorn. When I concluded that this compulsion had to change, I "shut the door" on it. But I didn't have to wait long to see what other doors opened for me to explore.

It seems like there is one game I haven't explored yet. It doesn't involve other players and doesn't seem like you could develop an obsession with it. It's the world of   Solitaire!   Now   that   might   be   harmless   fun.

A little slip on the ice, and welcome to ... Mister Toad's Wild Slide

It apparently happened overnight, because I certainly wasn't prepared for it. I just went to get the mail and soon found myself on the equivalent of Mister Toad's Wild Ride.

As I walked out from under my covered entryway and hit the sidewalk, I realized that during the night the erroneously romantic-sounding "silver frost" had occurred, and everything had been covered in a half-inch of ice. Sure, it makes for a beautiful sight, but I was using my cane then. It was all I had for brakes and rudder to navigate myself with, and frankly, it wasn't worth a darn for either.

About then, a gust of wind came up and turned my coat into something like big sails on a schooner ship, propelling me down the slippery walk. Since my house was on the high side of a downhill grade, the combination of wind, ice, and gravity sent me on my uncontrolled ride. As I started heading down my icy slide and realized my cane was really of no use, I made up my mind that there was no way I was going down.

Since my basic coordination (or lack of) didn't allow me to end this slick slide by just jumping off the sidewalk and onto the grass next to it, I knew I was going to have to get creative to end the ride. I saw a chance when I spotted a low tree limb that I could grab. The only problem was that I slid by it before I could grab it.

To keep my balance so I didn't crash, I found myself performing a series of Olympic-style ice skating moves. As I continued down the slope I saw my neighbor's hedge coming up next. All I would have to do to end my X-games ice marathon was somehow edge myself toward the bush and grab onto it.

In what I can only describe as some fantastic moves, which I'm sure included a couple of double axels (modesty prohibits me from exaggerating) that would have drawn praise from Dorothy Hamill, I finally was able to fall into the hedge.

As I gathered myself for my walk back on the more traction-friendly grass, I expected to hear cheers and applause for my wild ride on the ice... or at least the judges' scores. Nothing. Then I realized absolutely no one had witnessed this legendary athletic event.

I soon found out no one I told would believe me, and also they couldn't care less.

Even though I knew it happened – and it was pretty amazing – I realized trying to tell somebody else was the equivalent of telling them about "the big one that got away."

Now, let me tell you about the time I single-handedly stopped a possible ski disaster that no one else witnessed. It all started...

If only life were as right as rain

It's raining outside right now. Now that's not really strange or anything, but it's somewhat surprising considering that every weather forecast said that today would be mostly sunny, and about 70 degrees.

They didn't say it with even a twinge of doubt. It was declared with a certainty that you could count on.

As I sit here watching the rain, I wondered if that certainty could be applied to real life. I can hear it now. "I would have had the loan payment here this month, but because of usually reliable sources, I was told that a horse named Sunny Skies in the third race was without a doubt going to win that race. Because this information was given to me with such certainty, I bet all my money on it.

"Now the first two turns, I could see that my tip had been right, because that horse shot out of the gate like a bullet! Now I didn't know it was possible for a horse to suddenly get A.D.D., but it must be because suddenly the horse's attention went somewhere else, anywhere else but the race. With no apology, it came in dead last. Oh well, there's always next month."

I somehow don't think the bank would buy that.

Or maybe the next time I'm invited to a wedding, I can place a beautiful card on the gift table and write a note inside that says, "I had the perfect gift picked out for you two. As your wedding got closer, and it was time to buy that gift to help you start your new life together, I was suddenly hit with a surprise low system from the south that depressed my financial situation, making me unable to purchase that gift. Boy, that system seemed to really come from nowhere. Who could have predicted? I am sorry for the bad timing but be assured the best of thoughts are there."

Maybe I could get away with it if I said it with the same amount of certainty that the weather forecasters use. Regardless of how sincere I was, I somehow doubt that I would get a prompt thank you card, and possible invitations to a future open house probably would be out of the question.

Now, the weather forecasts are pretty accurate most of the time it seems, at least close enough that we always seem to watch them. But the certainty in which they forecast, or the confidence they have, must work somehow, because even when they're completely wrong, they're back smiling the next day without a hint of apology or explanation. You've got to admire that.

The funny thing is that the next time the forecast is for mostly sunny and 70 degrees, we'll still be surprised and somewhat forgiving when it's raining and only 50.

That's the one bright side to however the weather turns out. There's always someone who will like it the way it is and be glad that the forecast was wrong. Those people are always the quickest to be forgiving. Although, in the real world, I don't seem to be forgiven as quickly as the forecaster.

Oh well, the weather and even the poor weathermen always give us something to talk about. It's what seems to be an ever-changing constant. Nature providing something for someone to gripe about, free of charge. Now that's a bright side.

How much wood would a stubborn mule need?

At first I almost took it as a compliment. When someone said "You're as stubborn as a mule," I just assumed they meant that I was a person true to my beliefs and convictions, and not easily swayed. I took some pride in the statement until I realized that I shouldn't.

My father had a pet mule for 20+ years. When that mule decided he wasn't going to do something, no amount of pushing, pulling, poking, prodding or other forms of persuasion would make that mule change its mind. As I thought about it, I realized that this wasn't meant as a compliment. I think the kicker was when they also used the word "ass" (and I don't think they meant mule, or even a donkey) ... always an altogether great attribute.

As I wondered if maybe the bad side of that trait could pertain to me, I remembered a story my late aunt used to tell me. The church she went to as a small child had only a wood stove as its heating source, so the church had a woodshed.

There was a lady that rode her mule to church every Sunday. The lady would ride her mule and tie it up where all of the other horses, wagons, buggies, etc. were. She would then go inside to enjoy the church service. When it was all over, she would go to get on her mule for the mile or so ride home.

Now, when she was inside at the church service, the mule would lie down and go to sleep. When she tried to get the mule up for the ride home, it decided to show its stubborn streak. It had made up its mind- it wasn't going to get up. I guess it thought it could fall asleep at church too. This wasn't a one-time occurrence. In fact, it became a weekly ritual.

This became a real problem for the lady every Sunday. Getting tired of fighting that mule every week, she decided she would finally show it who was smarter. She would ride the mule right into the woodshed where she stacked wood under the mule so it couldn't lie down at all. Then she would go to church. When she came out to go home, the mule was standing. She would then move the wood from under the mule, get on, and ride home. She showed him!

I remember that story whenever I go to church, a wedding, a graduation or any other place where I might get the "nods" or wake myself up with a loud but inappropriate snort. (Come on, we've all done it!)

I'm not so stubborn as to not realize that I've been guilty of that before. Nowadays though I have a solution to my snoozing problem. Whenever I'm going to one of those possible situations, I just take a small piece of firewood to sit on. I might have more in common with that ass than I thought after all!

Who loves hot weather? Apparently everyone but me
And while we're at it, why assume we all adore ranch dressing?

I was really looking forward to watching the late news. In the "teaser" to get you interested in the newscast, the anchor excitedly urged viewers to be sure and watch later for some great news. Had the economy suddenly improved? Was a cure for cancer found? What could it be?

In great anticipation, I tuned in. While the whole crew looked giddy, the great news was ceremoniously revealed. It was going to be in the mid-80s tomorrow!

That's it? I stayed up to hear the great news for this?

Right then I finally realized (or at least admitted) that I was in a very small and much maligned minority, one that covered all races, religions, political beliefs, sexual preferences, age and generations. Apparently in the opinion of the majority, I should have believed that this was fantastic news. Well, I didn't.

My idea of a "perfect day" is a still, clear blue sky that's no hotter than 75. I admit it. I don't like summer, sun or hot weather. When I make that known, people treat me like I have leprosy or an extreme mental deficiency. But since I have big shoulders and can handle the taunts and discrimination, I can also admit that I function best when it's pitch black by 5 p.m.

There are a lot of things in this world people assume everyone likes. I can't understand why people automatically assume that everyone likes ranch dressing, yogurt or sour cream, or pretty much anything white. Mankind worked for centuries to find ways to keep and preserve food for safety and freshness. This has helped man to survive. Why, then, is it assumed that now, with a choice, everyone must like sour, spoiled tasting stuff? (I wonder: if the expiration date on sour cream passes, does it turn fresh?)

I could go on and on about things I don't like. Like all minorities, I too can't understand why others just don't accept these peccadillos. Even though I can't understand why anyone would eat something by choice that tastes spoiled, sour, or rotten, I don't pre-judge them for it.

As for those who say, "How do you know if you don't like it if you've never tried it?" Having lived for 60 years, if I died tomorrow not knowing whether I might develop a taste for spoiled food, I could certainly be happy with that.

Sorry, I just heard the timer on the oven go off, which means my meatloaf is done. I have to go enjoy an adventuresome, exotic meal complete with white bread, plenty of ketchup, mashed potatoes and mixed vegetables- all topped off with a vintage vanilla ice cream. Anyone else who belongs in this same minority, let me know. Maybe we can start a support group... or have a barbecue or something.

CHAPTER 5
WHEN DID I BECOME THE OLD GUY?

Tales of a computer illiterate: What, no floppy disk?

Now I've always considered myself of at least average intelligence, maybe wrongfully so, but I recently learned that I'm even more computer-illiterate than I expected.

My computer crashed. I found out it was infected with "viruses." How could this be? It never played with other computers, and I always washed my hands. I thought I took all the proper precautions, but apparently not.

After many failed attempts by others much more skilled than I to clean it up, it was decided that I needed a new computer. So off I went to the computer store.

As I walked into the store, I was bombarded by options, acronyms, and electric devices, most of which I had no idea what they were possibly for. I thought I felt my eyes glaze over. Then an overwhelming feeling of total ignorance scared me. I might as well have been asked to challenge the champion of "Jeopardy."

I went right to the cheapest computer, of course. When I told the sales person that I really only needed it for basic word processing and e-mail, I asked if it would handle the job. I figured even those basic terms made me look like I knew what I was talking about, right?

When the salesman started firing back terms such as "download," "burn CDs" and "transfer files," my face acquired a Gomer Pyle slack-jawed look. The salesman noticed my befuddlement, nodded in a patronizing way and said yes, it would do that.

I asked him where the floppy disk went, and he laughed at the question. "These new ones don't handle floppy disks. And why would you need to? But if you have to you can buy the option, for only $40 more, that can read floppy disks," he said.

Keep in mind that I had a floppy disk only because I was told in the not-so-distant past that it was the best way to go.

Then I realized I'd unknowingly entered some kind of weird lease program with the equipment I had just bought. Even though the computer was brand-new, it was as though I'd leased a car that already had 200,000 miles on it!

I also was paying for the "option" of a floppy disk reader that once upon a time was standard equipment – kind of like buying a car and paying for "optional" tires that already needed to be replaced.

Oh well. I guess the bright side is that I have time to save until my next lease payment comes due – I hope.

When did I become an 'old guy'?

It crept up on me, unnoticed, and I realized it had been going on for a while. I had become "the old guy." This really hit me when I noticed that I had reached the age where my doctors, lawyer, accountant and most everyone else I counted on for health and business information had become younger than me.

This became apparent when I was at the bank one day talking to a new loan manager. As we were discussing some business and financial matters, I suddenly had the sinking feeling that he was so much younger than me, he probably should be asking me if I would co-sign a loan for him to buy his first car.

I went to get a complete physical one day, expecting to see a wise and seasoned Dr. Marcus Welby type. Instead, in walked a kid who looked more like Doogie Howser or the kid I chased out of my yard a few years ago. When he finished the exam, he told me something I really didn't want to hear: "You're in pretty good shape for someone your age."

At first I was kind of insulted by that comment. Then I caught my reflection in the mirror and saw a guy who was about 40 pounds too heavy and definitely looked a lot older than I felt.

I knew things had changed when I actually caught myself enjoying a Lawrence Welk show rerun. When I was a kid we had no choice but to watch it and complained every time my parents turned it on. That show was for "old people."

I made my 10-year-old daughter watch it with me once. After about 10 minutes, when the audience was dancing, my daughter said, "Gee, Dad, this is just like 'The Muppet Show,' only with real people."

As I looked back, I realized this change didn't happen all at once. I can recall sounding like the "old guy" even years ago by saying some of the things I swore I never would, such as, "Because I said so!"

I guess that, as most 12-step programs claim, admitting you have a problem is the first step necessary to change. There are some things I can do so I don't become "the old guy." "Old guys" are about as popular as someone with a bad fever and hacking cough or infectious wounds.

One thing I've decided to never do is start a sentence with "I remember when..." or "You think that's bad, you should have seen ..." Neither one of those can ever end in conversation that's not going to bore or really irritate someone. Even if you do mention that you remember gas at 40 cents a gallon, or that the minimum wage was less than $2 an hour, nobody cares.

We all become "the old guy" eventually, but we can do some things to avoid that happening any sooner than necessary. Don't sound like one. Don't say things like "Well Ma, it's getting late, time to head for the barn."

Well, I guess I've had my little soapbox say. It's getting kind of late. It's almost time for the late news at 8 p.m., then off to bed. For some reason, morning just seems to come earlier than it used to.

'Why? Because I said so, that's why!'

(And you thought you'd never, ever sound like your parents ...)

It happens before you know it. Even though you say you will never do it, you start repeating the phrases that you were told as a child and swore you would never say to a child of your own.

You know, "Don't cross your eyes, they might stay that way" and "Shut the door, you're letting all the heat out!" "Money doesn't grow on trees" or "If all your friends jumped off a cliff, does that mean you would join them?" And of course, my favorite, "BEACAUSE I SAID SO!"

I'm sure you also have some of your own.

When you're younger, you don't understand the historical DNA that these statements have. They probably even go back to Adam and Eve, when she would say to Cain, "Don't tease Abel, someone could get hurt." (OK, bad example.) Probably from the time man first discovered fire and found that he could keep his cave warm, he was yelling at his son to shut the door.

I have never seen someone who was permanently cross eyed, but there probably was someone, somewhere, who was. To explain this to other people, someone probably said, "Oh, he crossed his eyes and they stuck that way."

These statements have continued through time. Some are virtually centuries old. Your great-great-grandparents said them to your great-grandparents, who then said them to your grandparents, and so on and so on. And now, whether you want to or not, you pass them on to your own children, who will one day pass them on to their children and so on and so on...

One time, when my daughter was 10, she and a friend wanted to go shopping at a mall by themselves. Of course I said no. My daughter said, "Wait a minute, Dad" (I knew just by that I'd better be on my toes), "Girls mature faster than boys, so actually we are more like 13."

I told her, "No, the way it works is that you are 10, so you're actually 10. If you were a boy, you would mentally be like 6 or 7."

That seemed to work, and I didn't have to use a single banned phrase.

Then it happened.

My daughter told me she wanted a new jacket that all her friends had, and it cost *only* $100. When I tried to tell her not to bow to peer pressure and to create a style of her own, she didn't buy that at all. I told her that money is not something you harvest or just pick up off the street. She didn't buy that either.

I was getting more frustrated and was running out of things to say. She said, "Dad, give me one good reason why I can't have it."

At a loss, I yelled, "BECAUSE I SAID SO!"

That actually worked. It was then I learned why some of the old classics work best, and I could see why they withstood the test of time.

Let me tell you about the good old days ... (and get off my lawn, punks!)

"You think this is bad..." "I can remember when..." "Back when I was younger..." "The price of gas was only 35 cents back in '68..."

When you hear a phrase like this, the people who say it act as though you're really interested (but you know it's really more for them than for whoever is listening). Ah, the good old days!

I guess when you get older, you lose any filter you have regarding what you say. Stories of the good old days always sound great because of how low prices were – but as in any story, there are two sides.

There is a great equalizer, and it's called minimum wage. Back in the "good old days," hamburgers at McDonald's cost only 19 cents, but minimum wage was $1.95 an hour. That meant you could by 10 hamburgers for one hour of work! Now, with minimum wage bumping $10 an hour, you can still buy 10 hamburgers at McDonald's.

Cigarettes cost only 99 cents a pack, or two for one hour's wage. In 1973, my rent for a brand new two-bedroom duplex with a washer, dryer and fireplace was $175 a month. If you compare that to $800 a month now, and to the minimum-wage increase of roughly five times what it used to be, the cost is still roughly the same.

The good old days! Just about everything else you compare works out about the same. People never seem to add that side of it.

If you constantly tell people about "the good old days" and go on about how great things used to be, how people are spoiled now, and so on and so forth, you soon will be known as the old man in the neighborhood who yells, "get off my lawn!" Before you know it, your house will stick out like a sore thumb on Halloween to all the trick-or-treaters. (And believe me, taking all that toilet paper off the tall maple tree out front takes a long time.)

You also don't want to talk about the dumb things you did. Back when the minimum wage wasn't that high, you paid more than $800 for a VCR and $600 for a microwave oven. A 21-inch color TV cost roughly $600, and you thought you were getting a good deal. You really don't want to add the fact that the last time you bought a microwave oven it was $39, or that a DVD player for your TV cost $74. You especially don't want to mention that you got a flat-screen, high-definition 32-inch TV on sale for $198. This kind of takes the wind out of all your "good old days" statements.

The lesson? The next time you buy something costly or pay a bill that you think is way too much, try to consider it this way: you are not paying too much for it now, you're just buying it to use in the future as evidence of how good things were in "the good old days." In a way, it's just an investment in making you the "get off my grass" guy.

Bad news from the doc: 'You have (gasp!) Dunlop's Disease'

I sat there and waited for the doctor to come in. I had gone in for a physical, and for some reason was nervous about what, if anything, he might have found.

When the doctor came in, he had a rather somber look on his face. He looked at the chart first.

"First of all," he told me, "both your lungs and heart look great, and overall, everything else looks fine."

As I started to relax, he said, "However, you unfortunately have an acute case of Dunlop's Disease."

Having never heard of this malady, I asked him what it was. He looked at me semi-seriously and said, "Dunlop's Disease occurs when your stomach has DONE LOPPED OVER YOUR BELT! There are only two kinds of proven cure and treatment. One is a strict regimen of diet and exercise; the other is to just buy a larger set of clothes."

As I was clothes shopping, I realized it could end up being expensive. Just when I was trying to figure out a way to increase my bank account, I saw a commercial by one of those "law firms" about class action law suits. If my second cousin's third wife was entitled to a settlement because her father's best friend was possibly exposed to asbestos, I figured I had a shot.

Finding a lawyer to handle this shouldn't be too hard; after all, I've seen the commercials where they almost beg people to find a connection to whatever cause they seem to have made up.

I can see it now: "If you suffer from Dunlop's Disease and have been exposed to cake, candy, pie, ice cream, chips of any kind, fast foods, pizza, brownies, sugary soda, beer, Hostess products (including Little Debbie), all-you-can-eat buffets, anything with a lot of butter or heavy cream, or basically anything that tastes really good, you too may qualify for a cash settlement!"

While they're at it, maybe the esteemed "law" firm Dewey, Cheatem and Howe can find some random doctor that says having been exposed to milk can cause baldness. It could be a latent form of lactose intolerance that develops later in life. Imagine how many people would jump on that one (I know I would!)

But I digress. While I was clothes shopping, I found a nice-looking shirt that didn't come in XXL. Really! That's a form of discrimination! There should be a lawsuit or something for such a slap in the face!

I guess 'Password' really is a game

It should've been easy. After all, I'd done it before. Even being severely "computer challenged" I was able to buy something on eBay before without any problems. Therefore, I thought this too would be hassle free.

I was looking for a portable ramp for my scooter. I easily went to the eBay website and quickly found the portable ramps. I found the one I was looking for, and the price was right. That was where the fun began.

With my debit card in hand, I confidently put my mouse on the "buy now" arrow. After being reminded that I was basically entering a legal contract, I fearlessly went on. I entered my card number as form of payment. Then, I was asked for my password.

Apparently, when I bought that $9 car poster about two or three years ago I had, unbeknownst to (or at least unremembered by) me, created a special password. After trying all the possible passwords I have used for other things, I still found that none of these were right. I finally clicked the button that asked "forgot password?" I was then informed that the information would be sent to my e-mail. That seemed easy enough! Maybe things wouldn't be that bad.

Sure enough, the next day I received a message from eBay. All my problems would be solved. I finally would be able to complete my purchase on the computer-like even a child can easily do. I opened the message. According to the e-mail, all I had to do to access all of my account information was to enter my password.

That was it. I called the 1-800 number on the site. After a few rings, a real person answered. They were more than happy to take my order immediately, and even gave me a tracking number. My order was complete and on its way, all in about 3 minutes!

I soon got another message from eBay. Because of the time that had elapsed between my order and a show of no payment, I had been put on "the list". I guess that meant those companies didn't want my business! That's alright, eBay wouldn't allow me to give it to them anyway. Must be a powerful password.

I got a final message from eBay reminding me about the contract I had entered into. To review the consequences and all the ramifications of it, all I had to do is enter my password! I figured the best thing for me to do was give up. I guess I'm just too old to figure out how to use eBay.

In the meantime, I'm searching for a class where I can become more 1-800 literate! It sure seems to be a lot easier.

You're offering me a WHAT discount?

It was like a sucker punch to the gut. Oh, I knew it would come eventually, but I sure wasn't ready for it. The situation took all I could muster to make myself feel better.

One night my sister-in-law asked if I wanted to go to Taco Bell with her and my niece and nephews. She added the magic words that were the ultimate deal closer: "I'll pay."

I said, "You bet."

What I thought would just be going to dinner soon became the equivalent of a mini-Twilight Zone.

"Just tell the girl what you want," my sister-in-law said to me as we stood at the counter. I ordered a chicken burrito and a small drink.

The girl repeated the order: "A chicken burrito and a senior drink."

Now I was only 49 at the time, and the word "senior" hit me like a plunge into an ice-cold pool.

"It is not a senior drink," I replied loudly.

"Be quiet – I'm getting a discount, and I'm paying," my sister-in-law said.

I told her, "Helen, I'll pay you a dollar more. It is not a senior drink!"

The words still hang in my mind with the persistence of a bad habit. It was the first time I had been offered any kind of discount for seniors. I wasn't a senior; my parents were.

When we got the food and returned to the table, my sister-in-law thought it comical that the 16-year-old girl at the counter thought I was a senior. The laughter soon dissipated when I pointed out that she probably also thought I was her husband.

With those words still ringing in my ears and tattooed on my brain, I thought to myself: there has to be a way to ease the sting of this almost surreal moment. I didn't think I looked old enough to be mistaken for a (gasp, choke) senior. I still had all of my hair, and none of it was gray. There were no other telltale signs that I could see.

I finally realized she must have offered me a chicken burrito and a *señor* drink. Anyway, that's my story, and I'm sticking to it.

I was pretty happy with how I was able to resolve the situation for myself and thought it was probably a one-time incident. Then about a year later it happened again.

I ordered my lunch at McDonald's, and as the girl was ringing up the total, the manager (this time she was about 30) said to the girl, "That's only $1.50."

Since I was ordering off the dollar menu and had received two items, I knew the total was $2. Wondering about the discrepancy, I made the mistake of asking why only $1.50.

"That's a senior Coke," she said.

This time the word stung like iodine on an open wound. I said, loudly and indignantly, "Excuse me, I'm only 50! How old do you think I am, and how old do you have to be?"

Embarrassed, she said, "There are no set rules, it's just a judgement call."

A judgement call? I certainly didn't feel like a senior, and it was hard to understand how anyone could possibly think I looked like one. I realized I had entered that netherworld between young and old – the world of discount haircuts and wearing stretch-waist pants while still working and having no grandkids. While white shoes that closed with Velcro and a myriad of other AARP-type products were available, I wasn't sure if I wanted to pursue them.

I decided I was not going to. I'd fight tooth and nail to not join my parents' peer group any earlier than possible.

Now you may wonder what could possibly be a "bright side" to this. Well, I learned a couple of things: pick and choose your fights, and cheapness is stronger than ego. Therefore, while I'm going to fight becoming a senior as long as I can and live life as young as I feel, I'm going to do it with half price Cokes from McDonald's.

Hair today... gone tomorrow

They just kept coming. I thought if I didn't open them or pretended the senders mailed them to me by mistake, they didn't exist. But no, I kept getting invitations to join AARP.

I realized they were right on the mark one morning when I looked in the mirror. I somehow had a lot more forehead than I remembered... I had to admit I was losing my hair. As much as it hurt, I decided there was no reason to try to hide it. Besides, hiding hair loss usually just draws more attention to it. Have you ever heard someone say, "Boy, that comb-over really looks good, where'd you get it done?"

With that in mind, I started just combing it back. But there was an intense glare on my forehead, so I started wearing hats more often to protect the eyes of passersby.

Then I noticed after having my beard trimmed one day that my beard grows much faster than my hair ever did. Women aren't the only ones who deal with gravity as they get older. I realized I wasn't really going bald, gravity had just made my hair fall. Instead of growing out of the top of my head, it was growing out of my chin.

I was also growing hair in new places. I now had hair in my ears, nose and a lot of places where it didn't exist before. That's a small comfort – when you start to contemplate selling advertising space on your newly available huge forehead, you'll take anything you can get.

The idea that men get more distinguished as they age is one notion that we can really grab onto. It's true that as a man gets older and starts to get gray around the temples he looks more handsome. That's not fair to women, I admit. Women spend millions of dollars to avoid looking old; if a man did that it would be spotted right away- even if you have the eyesight of Mr. Magoo.

When a man starts losing his hair, it's kind of like losing a friend you've seen every day of your life – a friend you really like but have to watch slowly go away, piece by piece. You can replace it with a toupee (some of which can be seen by Google's satellites), but it's not the same. It would almost feel better if your hair just said goodbye and left all at once.

Maybe this bugs me more than most. That must be because I'm more vain than a lot of men. At least I admit it.

I do agree though, women get the short end of the stick. At least men can show more skin when we go bald. As women get older, more skin is usually the last thing people want to see.

I guess in the grand scheme of things, losing my hair isn't really that bad. I finally joined AARP. Cuts down on my daily mail.

CHAPTER 6
HEALTH HUMOR

Calling Marcus Welby: Where are you

One night, for some unknown reason – or at least I forget why – I was stumbling around my pitch-dark living room. Since my basic mobility skills were questionable at best, what was soon to happen should have been expected.

I stubbed my toe on the leg of my couch.

I say stubbed because I can't think of a stronger word, and I really tried. Stubbed is much too tame of a word for how hard my toe slammed into that couch.

The fact that it was in total darkness and that it was a total surprise somehow made it hurt even worse. First, there was that microsecond before the brain really realized what happened, and then the true pain set in.

When the trauma of the situation finally hit me and I realized what had happened, I'm sure that a good amount of bad language was involved.

By the time I slowly got back to the light of my bedroom, my toe and foot had already begun to produce some remarkable and heretofore unseen colors. The next day, my toe and surrounding areas exhibited a colorful explosion of blues, purples and yellows. There were shades and colors that were completely new to me. If it weren't for the pain, and the fact that it was *my* foot, it would have kind of been a pretty sight.

I was sure that I had broken my toe, so I made an appointment with my doctor. I guess I had to confirm what I already knew. When I got to the exam room and removed my socks, my foot looked like the pastel color chart from the local paint store.

The doctor quickly confirmed what I already knew when he said, "You really did a good job on that one." After I was instantly comforted by that smooth bedside manner, I asked if there was anything that could be done for a broken toe. You know, such as wrapping it, a split, a cast, anything- even if it only made me feel like I was doing something.

"Not really," he replied. Again, in that soothing manner. Then he said something that gave me a tiny glimmer of hope. But that wouldn't last.

"Let's go get it X-rayed."

"What for?" I asked.

"So we can tell if it's a simple fracture or a compound fracture," he said.

I stupidly asked, "What's the difference?"

He then explained how if it were a simple fracture, it would feel better in about a week. If it were a compound fracture, it would take about two weeks.

"If it's a compound fracture, can anything be done?" I asked hopefully.

He said again in that ever-so-smooth tone: "Not really."

Well, in knowing what could be done either way, I told him, "I have a good idea. I'll call you in a week. If it feels better, we'll know it's a simple one. If it still hurts, then it's a compound one."

Since both were treated the same way, I realized it was a matter of time regardless of my diagnosis. We'll find out in about a week.

I guess that the bright side to all this is the fact that I saved the insurance company the cost of an x-ray (plus I saved me the cost of my deductible), and I was doing my small part to halt escalading, runaway medical expenses by being responsible for the fine care of doing nothing.

It all worked out, I felt better in about a week.

1-800-Dial-A-Doc-Or-Lawyer

I couldn't help but turn my attention to this one commercial that seemed to stick out from all the clutter of the rest. It seems that I may be entitled to money!

If I have been in an accident, whether in traffic, at home, at work, on a construction site or a vacation, or even if I've been bitten by an animal, I may be entitled to a settlement.

If that doesn't cover a broad enough area, I still may have a case. It seems that just being a witness to any of these may cause some sort of reimbursable mental trauma.

And there's always the commercial from the law firm looking for people who worked around asbestos, or people who knew people who may have possibly been exposed. If you even know of anyone, or have heard of someone who has, you could be exposed too! In fact, if you know anyone who can spell asbestos, you'd better call the 1-800 number right away. I think the firm's name was Dewey, Cheatum and Howe or something like that. I'm pretty sure they handled the woman who successfully sued for her coffee being too hot. And this was in front of a real judge and everything. They must be good.

I think these kinds of lawyers used to be called ambulance chasers. But since they're allowed to advertise now, being on TV somehow makes it seem more legitimate, or at least classier. Kind of gives all other lawyers a bad name.

I'm also tired of being bombarded by commercials that basically tell me I should know more than my doctor. After relating my symptoms, not only should I be able to diagnose my ailment, I should know what to prescribe. And to think my doctor went to 12-plus years of school... I learned it in 30 seconds! I now know the cure for restless leg syndrome, an overactive bladder, and underactive bladder, high cholesterol, erectile dysfunction, and even how to quit smoking.

Just keeping track of all these disorders has made me lose sleep; thankfully I now know what kind of sleeping aid I need and all of its possible side effects.

If thinking of all this sends me into a state of depression, I can also tell the doctor what I need to treat that. It's all enough to make me sit down and have a good cry of frustration, but I discovered I must have chronic dry-eye syndrome – one more thing on the list.

Now I'm not a sue-happy kind of person, but I'm tempted to sue the pharmaceutical company for its advertising turning me into an unpaid salesman for its products. Though I sell these products to myself, I get none of the financial benefits. They've also even made me imagine I have something I don't, and that I can diagnose myself instead of listening to my highly-trained doctor.

It's a case that would require a shrewd law firm, one that's good at going after companies with deep pockets, maybe even create a class-action lawsuit.

I think I know of a firm that would jump at handling this case. As a bonus, they even have a 1-800 number. How convenient!

Smoke-free and minty fresh (mmm, TicTacs)

The longest I ever really stuck to a resolution for my "own health" was about three months. I felt guilty for whatever bad habit I had and failing at fixing it made me feel even worse. So, to avoid the double pressure, I decided to quit smoking in the middle of summer. It was actually a birthday present for my daughter.

I had spent the past couple of years smoking the cheapest generic brand of menthol I could find, so I decided to go out with the best. I bought a pack of Salem Ultras and had my last cigarette. It was June 23rd, a Friday night at 11:27 p.m. (give or take) 14 years ago. After having smoked for 19 years, it was kind of like saying goodbye to an old friend (even if it was a spendy and irritating friend).

In those 19 years I had crept up to nearly two packs a day. I not only had developed a filthy, disgusting and increasingly expensive habit, but I also was becoming a social outcast. I had to do something.

I figured out the best tactic was to use TicTac mints. Only the white ones. I guess I thought they would cover up the smoke smell. Then I discovered that using two or three at a time, sucking them down about halfway, and inhaling deeply gave me a kind of "menthol" hit. I thought that was pretty cool. Maybe it would help me quit. I made up my mind I wasn't going to gain weight by eating candy or chewing on something bad for me all of the time. TicTacs had only one calorie apiece.

Whenever I had an urge to smoke, which was often, I would pop in some TicTacs. It seemed to work.

Before I knew it, I hadn't smoked in three weeks, but I had developed a four-or-five box of mints a day habit. People would ask me if I now realized how much better food tasted. To be honest, I had eaten so many mints my mouth was numb. I really hadn't tasted anything for a couple of weeks. Besides, I never thought food tasted that bad even when I was smoking.

Before I knew it, I had been smoke-free for a couple of months. I was buying TicTacs in 10 packs, like cartons. I found the mint habit much more socially acceptable, except that constant shaking sound whenever I moved. Oh well, better than smelling like smoke. Either way, people could always tell I was coming.

Over the past 14 years I have broken myself of TicTacs. Now I'm down to less than a pack a week. I still have a slight urge to smoke sometimes, but nothing that some TicTacs can't handle.

Besides the innumerable health benefits to quitting smoking, being more socially accepted, being allowed in the places that are more and more frequently becoming smoke-free, there's one true bright side: my clothes and breath smell minty fresh!

Why watching golf is bad for your health

It started out as a beautiful Sunday afternoon and I was going to enjoy my guilty pleasure of watching golf on TV. Now I say guilty because I don't play the game- I just enjoy watching those that do, and do it well. As I sat down and got comfortable, I was suddenly bombarded by some very disturbing commercials.

It seems that I could be suffering from a combination of both high blood pressure and high cholesterol. Not to worry. One pill can cure them both. I have to be careful though because it might interfere with other medication I'm taking. Better have my doctor look at it.

According to another urgent commercial I may be going to the bathroom too much at night. Again, only a doctor can tell, but if it's not some other more serious problem, there is another pill that can take care of that. Don't worry about the possible side effects- according to yet another "important message", those can also be taken care of by just a simple medication. Again- have the doctor check. (Why should I always have to ask, shouldn't the doctor already know?)

As I prepare my regular Sunday afternoon "watching golf lunch" of chips, a big bottle of Coke, and leftover pizza, I'm greeted on the TV by a grandfatherly looking man telling me that I can get all my diabetes supplies sent directly to my home. Now I don't have diabetes, try to generally eat right, and go to the gym 4 or 5 times a week. Nevertheless, it made me look at my once a week fat-fest ritual somewhat differently. Eh, somehow carrots and yogurt didn't quite seem the same. So far, all the commercials cast a depressing tone on what usually is a pleasant Sunday afternoon tradition that I look forward to all week.

No worries, my depression can be cured by some Zoloft. Or maybe I'm just allergic to these commercials- I need to be Claritin clear! I just can't operate heavy machinery, as it may cause drowsiness. If I have sinus pressure from all the allergies, I can also just take some Alka Seltzer Plus to handle that. So far, if I was a hypochondriac and worried about all this, I could take enough different pills and medication to glow in the dark. The first day of the tournament isn't even over yet and all these health commercials have ruined a good game of golf and left me with a headache. Believe it or not, there are several pills that will take care of that ailment.

At least all of this has made me realize that I have to do something about my health. It will take will power and sacrifice, but I'm going to start today. I'm going to quit watching golf!

Like a good neighbor ...

How I survived being hit by a car (yes, thank heaven, I have insurance)

I finally realized the time had come when I was making even myself nervous. After years of driving cars, buses, vans, semi and flatbed trucks, construction equipment, berry picking machines, and tractors of all kinds I came to the conclusion that it was time to turn in my license and quit driving.

When a simple drive had become a scary situation for me, I knew I better get off the road, not only for my own safety but for the safety of others. Unfortunately, what should have been a common-sense decision took a few vehicular mishaps and close calls for me to figure out. I made the decision to do this about two years ago, way past when I should have.

Thank God for good insurance. In fact, State Farm had almost become a welcome codependent. My driving skills (or lack of) cost them lots of money. Even though I paid my premium, and am well aware of the concept of insurance, I was almost starting to feel guilty about all the money they had paid. (Almost.) Now, by being off the road, State Farm could take my picture down from their wall of expensive, high-risk policyholders I imagine them keeping.

I turned in my license, quit driving and sold my van with hand controls. I was now completely grounded. Though giving up driving was a huge blow to my independence, I had to admit it also made me feel safer to not be taking risks on the road. It also made my daughter and others rest easy knowing I wasn't on the road anymore. The only thing I drove from then on was my three-wheeled electric scooter.

After two years or so, I was getting used to not driving and had learned the ropes of how to get most anyplace I wanted or needed to be.

Then it happened. I got hit by a car.

I was in the middle of a crosswalk when WHAM! Next thing I knew, I was being treated by paramedics who told me I had a broken leg, and off to the hospital we went.

At the emergency room I had a full set of X-rays and a CT scan; I found out that – miracle of miracles – the only thing really broken was my leg. It had broken in two places.

Other than that, I felt like I had been put in a sack and used like a piñata. I hurt everywhere.

I met my hospitalist – the doctor who oversaw my case, kind of a medical traffic cop. She told me an orthopedic surgeon would perform surgery to fix my leg.

The next thing I knew, I was wheeled into the recovery room. As I was adjusting to where I was and what had just happened, two nurses were right next to me talking to each other.

"Has the hospitalist been here yet?" one asked.

"No, I called, and the hospitalist will be here soon," came the other's reply.

Well, what *I* heard through my still-anesthesia-induced brain cobwebs was, "Has hospice been here yet?" "No, hospice will be here soon."

Yikes! My first thought was, "He said it was a routine procedure, and now they're calling for hospice!"

Well, I recovered fast. I don't know if the nurses' conversation was intended to speed up my recovery or not, but it sure worked. Just the thought of a visit from hospice cleared my head right up.

After five days in the hospital and five more at a rehab center, I went home. Now the healing and therapy start.

At least all this (hospital, ambulance, surgery etc.) is covered by the woman who hit me. I know from experience that she has a good insurance company. I don't have to worry as the bills pile up. She has State Farm.

If you need help, get it

People who have problems with mobility, walking, or balance all seem to share a common problem. For whatever reason, whether its denial or blissful ignorance, none of us seem to notice that any problem exists.

Even though I was using a cane at the time, in my mind, it just made me look pretty cool and somewhat debonair. One cold winter day I was reminded that I had it for a reason- even if I wasn't quite ready to admit it. Boy, was I about to get a (literal) cold slap in the face.

I went outside to check my mailbox across the street, using my cane with my usual swagger. When I got to the sidewalk, I could see it was covered in a thick coat of ice. Not good for someone with walking abilities that weren't so hot to begin with.

Then a strong gust of winter wind hit me and I began Mr. Toad's Wild Ride, the home version. Since the house was on top of a slight incline, I tried to use my ever-present cane to help stabilize me. Using that cane to steady my wobbly gait had about the same results as shooting pool with a rope.

I slid down that icy sidewalk totally out of control. When I tried to stop, I performed a maneuver that would make even a champion ice skater jealous. I thought, "I may be in trouble here."

It was then that I decided to stay on my feet. As I was headed down the sidewalk at what seemed to be breakneck speed, I spotted a way to stop. I was already down to the house beside mine when I saw a tree limb hanging over the sidewalk. I thought I'd just grab it and my ride would be over... no! I went by it faster than I saw it!

After some moves that better belonged in a gymnast's floor routine than on a sidewalk, I managed to stay upright on this killer slip-and-slide provided by Mother Nature. It was more than time to end this never-ending adventure. After sliding downhill a good 50 feet or so, I was still on my feet. But I knew my luck would run out, and I would soon only be able to rely on my questionable physical abilities. I knew I had to stop soon.

As fun as the ride had been, I knew I had to come to a *controlled* stop if I were to remain on my feet. This seemed to be important to avoid the pain that falling or tumbling on the cement sidewalk would surely cause. I've gotten to the age where falling's not nearly as fun as it used to be.

Finally I saw a possible end in sight. In the end of my neighbors' yard, next to the sidewalk, was a short (and thankfully dense) hedge. All I would have to do is somehow land against that hedge, and my impromptu standing luge would be over. While the details are unbeknownst to me, I was able to do just that, and I somehow stopped while still upright. I quickly looked around for judges' scores, or at least some sort of reaction from the non-existent crowd. Nothing. What a shame. (I couldn't repeat those moves on purpose even if I wanted to, and I really don't want to ever try.)

After those few out-of-control seconds of what seemed like physical mastery at the time, I realized two things. First, I really looked spastically ridiculous. Second, I risked my life and dignity because I denied what everyone knew. I had a serious mobility problem. I realized then that I needed more assistance than just that cane.

Afterward, I got the mobility aids I needed to make sure something like that hopefully wouldn't happen again. Pride be damned! The loss of a little self-perceived pride is better than loss of true blood.

Thank God, so far I haven't had to repeat my Olympic-quality performance. I got a three-wheeled scooter. It's not only a lot safer, but I also found that I look pretty dapper on it. I sure look better than stumbling around, trying to deny that I had a problem. That might only be my perception, but I realized that's the one that counts most.

The bright side? You still can look dapper and pretty cool with mobility aids, and you'll be a heck of a lot safer.

Behold the power and mystery of electricity

When I had the good fortune to be able to go to London, as always, I took my trusty three-wheeled travel scooter. Since England has a different power source than the U.S., I knew I had to take a plug adapter to be able to use my battery charger. I took several with me to be sure I had the right one.

I was able to take a friend with me, and after a very long flight we arrived in London. Everything was great, and my scooter, as usual, worked like a champ. We saw Buckingham Palace and a great outdoor market at Carnaby Square. We decided that the next day we were going to take the train to a coastal town called Brighton.

We stayed in a funky old bed and breakfast. The breakfast consisted of some white toast and strawberry jam. It had one bathroom down the hall for several rooms. But I digress.

By this time I needed to charge the batteries on my scooter. I had my charger and the correct plug adapters. I was all set, or so I thought.

I used the right adapter and plugged the charger into the wall, hooked it up to my battery on the scooter and prepared to go to sleep as the battery charged overnight. The plug went in all the way, but I noticed the meter on the charger was just bouncing back and forth. The little light on my scooter that shined bright green when the battery was charging was not on. Something was not working right.

I consider myself to be of at least average intelligence, so I said to my friend, "Something's wrong with the charger." Now my knowledge of electricity can probably fit into a thimble with room to spare, so the first thing I did was to pick up and shake the charger. Believe it or not, that had absolutely no effect.

Then I thought it must be the plug adapter, so I began to play with that. Again nothing. By now I was getting mad and frustrated. I kept trying different adapters and combinations until I somehow reached the wrong one. I ended up plugging the 120-volt charger directly into the 200-volt source.

If that means nothing to you, trust me – that was the wrong thing. There was an enormous loud crack and an intensely bright blue flash. I was thrown back away from the wall like a cartoon character, and a big puff of blue smoke came from the charger. I instinctively knew that this was not right.

Upon further inspection of the charger, even with my limited electrical knowledge, I quickly deduced that it was ruined. Maybe it was the smoke and the acrid burnt wiring smell that gave it away, but I knew it was ruined.

I didn't know what to do. I knew that without a charger I was up a certain creek without a paddle. As dependable as that scooter was, the battery charger was its life source.

Then my friend said, "Can't we charge the battery at an auto garage?" There it was! The bright side! The solution to a temporary bad circumstance!

We did just that, and it worked great. One charge lasted the rest of the trip. I learned later there is something called cycles as well as volts that kept the charger from functioning. Oh well, it all worked out.

We went on the train (they're not like our trains – when they say they're leaving at 4:07, that is exactly when they leave) to the coast and had a great day. The scooter would even drive right into the famous London black cabs. When the airport officials saw me on the scooter at Heathrow airport, he waived us past customs.

Even though I was blown against the wall like Wile E. Coyote in a Roadrunner cartoon while playing with my charger, the trip to England was more than worth it. Besides, I learned something: electricity is pretty mysterious. And I was right about one thing: the charger was toast.

Wheelchairs and escalators don't mix

I was at the Phoenix Airport after visiting my parents. As always on my travels, I was accompanied by my trusty three-wheeled scooter.

Now my travel scooter at the time was a basic, lightweight scooter that, even though extremely functional, was too small for me. Rolling along, I looked like an elephant straddling a sawhorse. Nevertheless, it got the job done.

I had to go up one level from where I was to catch my flight home. As I finally found the elevator I realized much to my chagrin that it was not working. A man from United Airlines saw me looking upset at the non-operating doors. "Someone will be right with you to give you a hand," he said, then he left.

Now I don't know if he meant someone would be there to fix the elevator, carry me up or what. I sat there looking dumb for a few minutes. I'm not really a carefree traveler to begin with, and I had a plane to catch in what felt to me like a few short minutes.

After waiting probably three or four minutes, I got (what seemed to be at the time) a brilliant idea. I'd take the escalator! Should be a piece of cake.

As I went around the corner there was an innocuous-looking escalator, and not a soul in sight waiting to get on. My lucky day. I would just ride up and get to the next level and catch my plane. Such a simple plan – I was surprised that no one had done it before.

I was soon to find out why.

I drove my scooter onto the empty, seemingly harmless, slowly ascending stairs. As the first level of stairs went up, I was even more convinced this was a brilliant idea. As the second level went up, I was feeling pretty cocky. When the third step rose slightly into view, all hell broke loose.

The scooter went straight up into the air and dumped me out. As I was flung backward, the handlebars, the only easily removable part on the scooter, hit me square in the chops.

For some reason, I thought to myself, "These are stairs. I'll just slide to the bottom and then walk up." I was quickly reminded it was indeed an escalator as I felt the new steps rising on the back of my head.

When I realized (after being smacked in the head) that these were not stationary stairs, I thought, "OK, I just kind of ride it up to the top. No problem."

That plan was working all right until I was heading to the top and happened to look. Somewhere in the execution of this "brilliant" idea, I must have thought that the scooter, which was standing straight up, would gently lower itself down at the top and easily roll off the escalator.

I hadn't realized that at the top, the scooter would stay there while the moving steps would roll nicely under the back wheels of the upturned vehicle. "This may be a problem," I thought.

As I got closer to the top and to the scooter, I realized my only chance was to kick it up as I approached the top. In what I envisioned as a carefully choreographed, almost ballet-like, movement, I kicked the scooter forward, rolled off the top of the moving stairs, gathered the pieces of the scooter together and went on my merry way. (I realize now that I probably looked more like an uncoordinated turtle trying to roll off its back.)

What surprised me is that when I started riding the escalator, no one was in sight. By the time it took me to reach the top, there were at least 25 people waiting at the bottom to come up.

On my flight home, I hurt as though someone had beaten me with a big stick. "No wonder this hasn't been done before," I thought.

The incident confirmed what I had learned in third grade about the law of nature called gravity. Take my word for it: the concept works. So the next time you see that small sign on the side of an escalator that says, "No strollers or wheelchairs allowed," it does mean *you.*

Feeling low? Picture a cow on a walker

First of all, a little background on this story. When you're first diagnosed with multiple sclerosis, friends will always tell you about some miracle treatment they've heard about and how it cured someone. These are all offered with the best of intentions.

Unfortunately, MS and its symptoms can go into remission or even sometimes disappear, for a while or even forever, depending on the type of disease one may have. This makes it difficult, if not impossible, to tell the effectiveness of a treatment- whether traditional or alternative in nature. Therefore, you can endure even the most bizarre treatments (for me, the thought of bee stings) for a long period of time, only to find out eventually they had no effect.

One night, a friend called me all excited. He had just read about a new treatment for MS and thought I should look into it. Apparently, scientists had somehow replicated MS in cows. I believe the theory was that the lactate in the milk would create antibodies, and drinking the milk from these cows could help MS in humans.

As it turned out, the validity of the trials for this treatment lasted about two weeks. But in the meantime, my friend was excited about what he had read.

Shortly after he called me, I went to the annual MS Symposium that is sponsored by the Oregon Chapter of the National MS Society. It is a meeting to show off the latest medical treatments, insurance programs, physical therapy, durable goods, etc. that are available for those with MS. I always took a trade table and extolled travel for the mobility impaired.

In between the many sessions we stopped for lunch. At the table where I was eating, there was a girl about my age. She was in a wheelchair, and I could tell by looking that she probably hadn't had a really good laugh in years.

It was easy to see why. Her mother was there asking others if they had tried copper and magnetic bracelets around their ankles, bee stings, acupuncture, etc.

Now there isn't anything I wouldn't do to help my daughter either, but I could tell that the girl was somewhat browbeat by her caring, loving, somewhat overbearing mother.

As I sat across from her, I explained what my friend had told me. I asked her if she had tried drinking that milk. Her eyes got wide:

"No, have you?"

"No way" I replied.

"Why not?" she asked me.

"Get the picture in your mind. The farmer calls the cows in to milk, and over the hill come 50 cows with MS in wheelchairs or walkers and bumping into trees! I don't think I want to drink that!"

The girl almost fell out of her chair laughing, while her mother said, "That's a terrible and awful thing to say."

I just looked at her and said, "Ma'am, if you can't smile at the mental picture of a cow on a walker, you have more problems than your daughter and I put together!"

Whenever I'm feeling kind of down or need a good laugh, I picture a cow on a walker or negotiating a wheelchair. It works every time.

How I found power in a wheelchair

It wasn't as easy as it always looked, and the carpet was much thicker than I thought. I'd been out of the hospital for a while after having been diagnosed with multiple sclerosis.

My then-wife decided it would be good for me to get out of the house and go shopping with her and my sister-in-law and niece and nephew. Since I couldn't walk very far yet, we borrowed an old wheelchair from the local Elks club.

I was pushed around, and everything was great until they went into a store I really didn't want to go into. I wanted to go into one that was at the other end of the mall. While I was waiting for them, I decided I would just push myself. Shouldn't be that hard, or so I thought...

As I pushed myself along that thick carpet (which took more strength than I expected), I noticed that people in the mall were looking at me. They were either wondering what a young, big guy like me was doing in a wheelchair, or watching me huff and puff going down the mall. Either way, I was drawing attention.

Now I've never been adverse to attention. In fact, I've been told I sometimes go out of my way to attract it. So when I saw the people's somewhat puzzled look, I slumped a little bit to add to the questions they already had. It was pretty funny.

I finally worked my way up the length of the mall and got to the store, attracting more onlookers all along the way.

When I got to the entrance of the store, there was a threshold that stopped me like a brick wall. The bump was hard to get over, and the think carpet made it extra difficult. I backed the chair up and tried again, and again I came to a sudden stop. One more time – again, nothing. I noticed out of the corner of my eye that I was attracting even more seemingly concerned onlookers.

This time I said quite loudly, "SON OF A B----!!", got up, picked up the chair and put it over the threshold, then got back in it, slumped again and again slowly pushed away.

I looked back, out of the corner of my eye. All those people were now looking with total surprise. They looked like deer caught in headlights.

I should have felt guilty, but I thought it was kind of funny. Right then and there, I realized even though I had no control over being in the chair, I could control how others thought of me. Kind of a bright side in a back-handed way.

As selfish as it was, I found that I could use the chair to my advantage; sometimes I'm the only one who found it funny. But at least I was in control. Pretty cool.

If you look hard enough, you can find a bright side to most any situation you might be in. If not, make one up, especially if you need a smile. Remember, you're in control.

The upside to being in a wheelchair

It wasn't a real deluge – just that kind of solid light rain that got everything good and wet. As I circled the parking lot at the mall, I was glad to see that handicap-parking spot right by the front door.

I pulled in, and as I unloaded and got out, I couldn't help but feel kind of sorry for everyone else. They had to get a soaking as they walked clear across the parking lot to get inside. I couldn't help but smile smugly to myself.

Now I don't know anyone who chooses to be in a wheelchair. But since I didn't have any say in the matter, I soon decided that since I was, I might as well make the best of it. I didn't have to look too hard to find some good things about it. They were just right there.

The first time I realized there may be some unknown benefits to this was when I was diagnosed and just borrowing a chair. I found out that if I worked it right, the attention it drew was pretty cool. Now I kind of like attention anyway, so maybe I just imagined that. Either way, I'll take it.

It definitely can be a benefit when shopping, especially if you have a power chair like mine. You can go from one end of the mall and back again and not really be tired. It never fails, though- sooner or later, some overweight lady (usually with over-bleached hair) sucking on a Big Gulp will say, "I sure could use one of those, my feet are killing me," to which my standard reply is, "Well, my butt really hurts, and it's bigger than your feet!" At least I get a good laugh out of it.

One benefit that you would never suspect are free periodic hearing tests. Sooner or later somebody will come up to me and say quite loudly, "CAN I HELP YOU?" It seems that because my legs don't work, my hearing must not work, either. If it sounds really loud to me, I figure my hearing must be all right. Still can't walk, but I can hear someone sneaking up on me as I roll along.

I'm much better read since I started using my wheelchair. Especially in grocery stores. Because I'm sitting in line at the checkout stand, it allows more time and a better view to read all the tabloid headlines. Just knowing them, true or not, makes me sound up on things.

Other benefits: those automatic door openers are pretty cool, and my power chair is a really handy place to stack and carry packages – I can look like a parade float at the mall around Christmastime.

Oh, did I also mention really good parking?

10 things I likely will never hear

I couldn't help by laugh. It might have been sad if it weren't so funny to think about. I was asked if I would participate in a fundraising fun run. Since I came down with multiple sclerosis 30-plus years ago, I've slowly lost a lot of physical abilities and haven't run, let alone walk, in 10 years.

By thinking of the funny aspects of this, I was able to find the bright side. Since this has been a good way for me to deal with the inevitable changes, I sat one night and thought of some things I won't hear and ways to find the bright side of them:

10. Hey, will you help me move next weekend?

9. Will you hold the baby while I run to the store?

8. Feel how heavy this antique china teapot is that my great-grandmother left me.

7. You chopped all that wood today?

6. Runners, take your mark.

5. Do you use free weights or the Nautilus machine?

4. That motor really hums since you rebuilt the carburetor!

3. Are you sure this calligraphy wasn't done professionally?

2. You mean this finely detailed wood carving was done with just one knife?

1. Wow, who taught you how to dance? I thought I was watching Fred Astaire!

Missing out on most of these things is not a terrible tragedy. In fact, never getting asked to help a friend move is something of a blessing. This can be seen as a kind of backhanded bright side. Bright sides are always there – sometimes you just have to look for them.

For example, one advantage of being bald is that you never have a bad hair day. You also never have to worry about knowing when to stop washing your face and start shampooing your hair.

If you're a little bit overweight, tell people it's power flesh. It can come in handy if you ever have to throw your weight around.

If you're kind of uncoordinated, just explain that anyone can be coordinated or a good athlete, but you're building character instead of muscles by taking the road less travelled.

Wallet a little thin? You too could be financially successful, but you just don't want all the pressure. Plus you're less likely to get robbed.

As you can see, almost any situation can be given a spin to help you better deal with whatever circumstance you've been handed. By finding the bright side, you're in control! Like I said, the bright side is almost always there if you just look – or sometimes even invent it.

If you have anything that you will probably never hear to add to this list, let me know.

Saved from the lions' den

The sky was a beautiful blue, and the warm summer breeze was flowing. Right after I'd been diagnosed with multiple sclerosis, I'd been inside for way too long and was starting to feel a little gray. My wife and sister decided I should get outside and came up with the idea of going to the zoo. That sounded great to me. Little did I know how great.

At the time I wasn't using a wheelchair day to day, and we'd returned the one we had borrowed from the Elks club. Because of the hills at the zoo, and its size, we borrowed one of theirs. That wheelchair was one of those molded fiberglass chairs mounted on a pipe and metal frame with small wheels. It could only be pushed; the rider could not control it at all. That was OK with me because all I had to do was sit there and enjoy the ride and savor the view.

My wife and sister pushed the chair together around the park. After wandering around the penguins and reptile exhibits, we were at the top of a slope heading towards the lions.

"Wouldn't it be funny if we let go of him?" one of them commented. They got to laughing so hard, they did just that. They both took their hands off the grips, and I found myself building speed until I was eventually careening down the hill headed toward the lions' exhibit (actually, quickly rolling, but for drama and the story, careening sounds a lot better).

The way the exhibit was constructed made sure I couldn't have gotten in if I'd tried, and the 10-inch-high concrete barrier before it made it impossible to roll in. But at the time, as I was careening (or quickly rolling) toward those lions, I was thinking what the headlines would say the next morning: "MAN IN WHEELCHAIR MAULED TO DEATH BY HUNGRY LIONS!"

After my wife and sister regained their wits and some semblance of composure, they caught up with me against the curb and the metal railing of the lions' case. We went on and enjoyed the rest of the zoo, but they giggled at every hill that day, and I was somewhat nervous.

All in all, that experience made the trip a little more memorable. While I was rolling uncontrolled toward the lions, I not only completely forgot that I had just been diagnosed with a weird disease, but I realized that things in general could have been a whole lot worse. Thank God for that 10-inch curb and metal railing.

As we headed home, I suddenly felt pretty darn good.

Pureed (Not) to Perfection

I was wondering how they could possibly could do this. As I was soon to find out: not too well. I was on a pureed food only order when I was in the hospital, and one of my breakfast choices was pureed French toast! I had to order it to see how they took a piece of basically dry bread and pureed it so it would be soft and have the consistency of vanilla pudding.

What turned up on my plate the next morning looked more like a used yellow kitchen sponge (that wasn't even square) than the golden brown, powdered sugar dusted, syrup drenched beauty straight off the menu of the local pancake house. At least that's what I had expected in my mind. So was the start of my puree-only restricted diet.

The French toast was only the start. It actually got worse from the very beginning. My mind has forgotten what my choices were for lunch. I must have had some form of protective amnesia because maybe they were as bad as the breakfast. Or maybe I just forgot.

I do remember my dinner choices though. They were limited to what was described as basically beef, chicken, or pork dinners. My first choice was the chicken. It was described in the menu as "roast chicken breast with select garden vegetables and mashed potatoes". "Not bad," I thought. It sounded like a good choice.

When dinner came that night, I was looking forward to my selection. I opened the tray in eager anticipation. What I found was exactly what was described on the menu. Except for one thing. Nowhere did it mention that all these delectable sounding ingredients would be dumped together in one big blender and put on the "puree" setting for God only knows how long. What resulted was a pile of warm, indiscernible "food" that was somehow passed off as what was so eloquently described on the menu. Must be a mistake, or maybe just a bad day. I'd give this puree menu another shot.

This time I'd try the "succulently tender, moist roast pork with fresh green beans". Unfortunately, the day before wasn't a mistake or just a bad day. The results were the same. And surprisingly enough, they tasted exactly the same, even though one was supposed to be chicken and one pork! The flavors were indistinguishable, except that neither was good.

I had one more dinner try, "roast beef with roasted carrots". Hopefully this would somehow taste differently. I'd pretty well written off the fact it would be of any different consistency. It was, after all, a puree restricted diet. By now I'd accepted that. I'd just hoped that they would somehow taste just the least bit differently.

I opened the cover kind of slowly and peeked in, as if that might make a difference. What I saw was the same pile of mixed food, but over on the side by the requisite mashed potatoes were THREE WHOLE CARROTS! My heart jumped in anticipation. Actual real whole, cuttable, maybe crunchy food. And I liked carrots. Even if I hadn't, I still would have been excited. Finally, something with a different taste, at least a different texture! I couldn't wait!

I bypassed the beef knowing what it was going to taste and feel like and went straight for the carrots. I wanted to savor the moment. I picked up my fork to slice the carrots. My mouth watered. I slowly cut the carrots with my fork. Finally! As I cut them, I realized that my fork went in much too easily. The carrots were PUREED also!

But wait a minute. These were definitely three roast carrots. Now there was just an orange pile. On further inspection, I realized that they had used a formed press to make the pureed, whipped orange mess look like whole carrots! I guess they thought if the mind was fooled, so your mouth would be too. For a brief second it almost worked. They were just a pile of orange, mashed carrots. Somehow if something is pureed, it has its own flavor, and they're all the same. I finally gave in to the fact that this was my fate until I was off this dietary restriction.

The bright side to all this? The next time I'm at a potluck, someone else's home for dinner, or even a restaurant, if I didn't like it before but it's whole and recognizable, chances are it's going to be DARNED GOOD! Comes in pretty handy.

Made in the USA
Middletown, DE
11 January 2019